THE MIND AND ITS CONTR[illegible]

Swa[illegible] udhananda

Advaita Ashrama
(Publication Department)
5 Dehi Entally Road
Kolkata 700 014

Published by
Swami Bodhasarananda
President, Advaita Ashrama
Mayavati, Champawat, Uttarakhand
from its Publication Department, Kolkata
Email : mail@advaitaashrama.org
Website : www.advaitaashrama.org

First Edition, 1971
Twenty-seventh Impression, June 2007
16M3C

ISBN 81-7505-034-9

Printed in India at
Trio Process
Kolkata 700 014

PREFACE TO THE FIRST REPRINT

The first edition of *The Mind and Its Control* having gone out of print much earlier than expected—within five months of its publication—we are now reprinting it with a few improvements here and there in the text.

It is likely to be increasingly realized everywhere in the world that man's well-being is inseparable from mind-control. Hence we hope that the circulation of this small book will steadily widen.

Advaita Ashrama THE PUBLISHER
Mayavati, Himalayas
February 16, 1972

PREFACE TO THE FIRST EDITION

The control of the mind is a theme of universal interest. It personally concerns every spiritual seeker belonging to any religion. Religion in its applied aspect has to grapple with this problem. No fundamental work for the uplift of the individual or the community can ever be done without mind-control. Hence its compelling claim on our attention.

Among those who seek to control their minds

there are different kinds of people: atheists, believers, agnostics, and those who are indifferent to religion. Ways of controlling the mind are open to all these kinds of people, though the true believer in God may be at an advantage in that genuine love of God can to a considerable degree simplify his problems with the mind. This book, however, is written for all. A detached inquirer will keep his mind open to all the methods of controlling the mind.

Vedanta and Yoga have much to teach about the nature of the mind and the ways of controlling it. In his treatment the author has largely depended on such information and enlightenment as the authentic scriptures and teachers of Vedanta and Yoga provide.

The Mind and Its Control was first serialized in the 'Essays on Applied Religion' column in the October, November and December 1970 issues of *Prabuddha Bharata*. It attracted the attention of some readers, one of whom generously offered to contribute towards the cost of its production as a book for wider circulation. Our thanks are due to that friend.

In this publication the text of the original article has been revised; certain points have been further elucidated; and some points have been added. A summary and glossary have been provided.

It is hoped that this small book, which addresses itself to one of the central problems of life, may be of service.

Advaita Ashrama
Mayavati, Himalayas
September 30, 1971

THE PUBLISHER

CONTENTS

1

MIND-CONTROL: DIFFICULT BUT POSSIBLE

In this theme, the mind and its control, we are all deeply interested, in a very personal way, for nothing affects us individually more than our own minds. We know something about the subject. All of us try to control our minds. But we should like to know more and do better.

Who can help us in this regard? Only those who have perfectly controlled their own minds. What we may learn from such sources we shall present here as a system of simple disciplines.

Control of the mind is a very interesting inner game. If you have a sportsman's attitude you will thoroughly enjoy it, even while apparently losing. In the playing, this game takes a great deal of skill, alertness, sense of humour, goodness of heart, sense of strategy, patience and some heroic flair which makes it possible not to get disheartened in the face of a hundred failures.

Śrī Kṛṣṇa was explaining in the *Gītā* how the supreme state of Yoga was to be attained. After listening to him Arjuna said to the Lord in understandable despair:

O Kṛṣṇa, this yoga which you declare to

> be characterized by perfect evenness of mind, I do not see how it can endure, because of the restlessness of the mind.[1] The mind, O Kṛṣṇa, is restless, turbulent, powerful and obstinate. To control the mind is as hard, it seems to me, as to control the wind.[2]

Śrī Kṛṣṇa listened to this representative complaint of man and gave a reply important for all men of all times. All Indian thinking and practice on mind-control are largely based on this teaching of Śrī Kṛṣṇa. He said: 'Undoubtedly, O Arjuna, the mind is restless and hard to control. But by practice (*abhyāsa*) and dispassion (*vairāgya*) it can be controlled.'[3]

From this conversation we know three basic facts about mind-control:

a. That it has always been an extremely difficult task even for heroic persons of the stature of Arjuna.
b. That yet it is possible to control the mind.
c. That there are well-defined methods for controlling the mind.

In these two words, *abhyāsa* and *vairāgya*,

---

[1]VI. 33.
[2]VI. 34.
[3]VI. 35.

practice and dispassion, Śrī Kṛṣṇa gave the whole secret of controlling the mind.

It is the uniform verdict of all the saints of India down the ages that there is no other way of controlling the mind except through 'practice and dispassion'. This is also called '*abhyāsa-yoga*' or 'the yoga of practice'.

We shall quote here a dialogue between Sri Ramakrishna and a devotee, in which the former emphasizes a fundamental point which everyone needs to remember:

> Sri Ramakrishna: 'Don't sit idle simply because your spiritual consciousness had been awakened a little. Go forward. Beyond the forest of sandal-wood there are other and more valuable things—silver-mines, gold-mines and so on.'
>
> Priya: 'Sir, our legs are in chains. We cannot go forward.'
>
> Sri Ramakrishna: 'What if the legs are chained? The important thing is the mind. Bondage is of the mind, and freedom is also of the mind.'
>
> Priya: 'But the mind is not under my control.'
>
> Sri Ramakrishna: 'How is that? There is such a thing as *abhyāsa-yoga*, yoga through practice. Keep up the practice and you will

> find that your mind will follow in whatever direction you lead it. The mind is like a white cloth just returned from the laundry. It will be red if you dip it in red dye and blue if you dip it in blue. It will have whatever colour you dip it in.'[4]

Practice and dispassion are no doubt the entire secret of controlling the mind. But how do we bring them into our life-stream? That is the question. To do this

a. we shall have to develop a strong will to control the mind;
b. we shall have to understand the nature of the mind;
c. we shall have to learn certain techniques and practise them earnestly and intelligently.

---

[4]'M', *The Gospel of Sri Ramakrishna*, tr. by Swami Nikhilananda, (Chennai: Sri Ramakrishna Math, 1964), p. 499.

2

HOW TO STRENGTHEN THE WILL TO CONTROL THE MIND

It cannot be said that we have no will to control the mind. The very fact that all of us have our own inner struggles indicates that we have the will. But in most cases this will to control the mind is not very strong.

Our will to control the mind can never be strong until and unless we have deliberately and irrevocably renounced pleasure as one of the main pursuits of our life. The canker which eats away the vitality of our will to control the mind is the pursuit of pleasure. It is like this: if you have a servant who is aware that you depend on him to procure you illicit drugs and if you both enjoy the drug together, you cannot then control that servant. The same is the case with the mind. The mind which we use for seeking pleasure and enjoying pleasure, we can never control until we give up seeking pleasure. Even after giving up the pursuit of pleasure it will not be easy to control it for the mind will always have past incidents to cite to embarrass us. The strength of our will to control the mind will be in proportion to the strength and intensity of our renunciation of the pursuit of pleasure. Unless the pleasure-motive is overcome, no matter what else we do, we can never perfectly control the mind. The derivative of this truth is that those who are reluctant to renounce the pleasure-motive are not sincere enough in wanting to control their minds, whatever their professions.

By renunciation of the pursuit of pleasure is not meant renunciation of the pursuit of joy or bliss. By pleasure is meant the enjoyment of sense-pleasures or the gratification arising from what Sri Ramakrishna calls the 'unripe ego', both of which obstruct the attainment of joy or bliss. It is by going beyond pleasure and pain that one attains joy or bliss, which is the very goal of life. There is no question of giving up the desire for joy or bliss, for it is integral to us, our real nature being Existence-Knowledge-Bliss. About the method of overcoming the pleasure motive something will be said in the next section.

Opposites sometimes look alike. Two types of persons do not have inner struggle; those who have become unquestioning slaves of their lower nature, and those who have completely mastered their lower nature. All others have inner struggles, which are the result of inadequate or unsuccessful attempts at controlling the mind. Inadequate attempts are indications of weak will and of lack of knowledge as to how to control the mind.

The most important thing is to strengthen the will to such a degree that even in the face of repeated failures we are not disheartened; rather, that with every new failure to control the mind we are roused to fresh endeavours with new enthusiasm.

Now how do we strengthen this will to control the mind? We have to remove the causes of weakness of will. And we have to inject strength into it by ensuring the presence of suitable causes.

No doubt some of us have struggled with our minds but have faced repeated failures. So we have come to believe that controlling the mind is not for us. Another reason for the weakness of our will is that most of us have perhaps not clearly thought what exactly is at stake in the control of the mind. If we had, the sheer instinct for survival would have driven us to strengthen our will to control the mind. As regards our failures to control the mind, we need not be unduly exercised. It has never been an easy task even for the noblest of men, the nature of the mind being restless. Śrī Kṛṣṇa says in the *Gītā*:

> The turbulent senses, O Arjuna, do violently snatch away the mind of even a wise man, striving after perfection.
>
> For the mind which follows in the wake of the wandering senses, carries away his discrimination, as a wind carries off its course a boat on the waters.[5]

---

[5] II. 60 and 67.

The Buddha teaches:

> If one man conquers in battle a thousand men a thousand times, and if another conquers himself, he (the latter) is the greater conqueror.[6]

From this we can understand that controlling the mind is the most difficult task in the world. It is indeed a hero's task. Hence occasional or repeated failures to control the mind should not be taken too seriously. Failures should be taken as spurs to more determined, sustained, and intelligent efforts, for we are assured by the great teachers that perfect control of the mind is possible. All thoughts to the contrary must be eschewed like poison.

3

WHAT IS AT STAKE IN CONTROLLING THE MIND

We must clearly understand what is at stake in controlling the mind. Insanity is the worst thing that can happen to an individual as a result of non-

---

[6]*Dhammapada*, verse 103.

control of the mind. Collectively, non-control of mind may lead to the downfall of an entire civilization, however prosperous or stable it may appear to be. There are many other lesser misfortunes that directly or indirectly issue from non-control of mind.

Non-control of mind effectively obstructs integration of personality. A person of uncontrolled mind will always have a tendency to abnormal developments or to mental disintegration through internal conflict. Even under the most favourable circumstances he will not realize his potential or fulfil expectations.

One who has no control over his mind cannot have peace of mind. One who has no peace of mind, how can he have happiness? A victim of passions, emotions and tensions, he may develop obstinate mental maladies or turn into a criminal. If he is the head of a household, indiscipline, disorder, delinquency, and wretched human relationships leading to family misfortunes are likely to prevail.

In an Indian maxim it is said: a man may have received the grace of God, of the teacher and of holy men; but if he does not have the grace of his own mind he will go to rack and ruin. Having the grace of one's own mind means having control of it.

On the positive side, at its highest, through control of mind one can attain spiritual illumination. Short of that there are many other blessings of life attainable through control of mind. A controlled mind can easily be concentrated. Through concentration of mind one gains knowledge. And knowledge is power.

One of the spontaneous results of control of mind is integration of personality. Such a person succeeds, even in adverse circumstances. A controlled state of mind leads to calmness, and calmness leads to peace of mind. Peace of mind leads to happiness. A happy person makes others happy. The quality of his work improves steadily and he often attains enduring prosperity as a matter of course. It is not that such a person has not to face the trials and tribulations of life. But he never lacks the courage and strength to face them. At home, where he is the head, there are greater chances of order, discipline, joy, culture, and excellent human relations. Society looks upon such a person as an exemplar of good life.

A person of controlled mind will be free from mental maladies and physical troubles caused by mental tension.

In a person who has controlled his mind his higher nature asserts itself, and his hidden powers are released. Friends wonder how this person could become, before their eyes, so great. A popular Sanskrit maxim says: 'Who conquers the world? He alone who conquers his mind.'

Progress, prosperity or peace—nothing of an

enduring nature can be achieved in any field without control of mind. People without self-control will not retain even the prosperity that they have.

Such are the stakes in control of the mind. To develop a strong will to control the mind, we must teach our own minds that, without it, we are nowhere. We must impress upon ourselves the fact that the character of our entire future depends on whether or not we control our minds. After fulfilling man's basic physical needs, other things also may be important; but for the attainment of the highest objective of life—spiritual illumination—nothing in life is more important than controlling the mind. Once we really understand and believe this, our will to control the mind will become strong, as strong as we need to have it.

4

HOW TO OVERCOME THE PLEASURE-MOTIVE

We have said: 'Unless the pleasure-motive is overcome, no matter what else we do, we can never perfectly control the mind.' This statement may give a rude jolt to many who struggle with their minds. But it is a statement of fact, and the implications of this fact need to be grasped.

It is easy to say bluntly that unless the pleasure-motive is renounced one cannot have a strong will to control the mind. But the pleasure-urge, being elemental in us, is so deeply ingrained in our flesh and blood that it can be got rid of, if at all, only with the greatest difficulty. We must not, however, complicate our inner situation by imagining that we are wicked in seeking pleasure. The pleasure-motive is not in itself sinful, though, of course, indulgence in immoral pleasures which create greater bondage and retard our higher self-development, is. Except for a microscopic minority—who, in response to a higher call, have renounced worldly pursuits and about whom we are not speaking here—except for them, life itself will hardly be possible without some satisfaction of the pleasure-urge. 'What to live for, if not for pleasure?' will be the honest question of the majority of mankind. This urge is a living force in man, and a force by which he lives. Yet it is true that the pleasure-motive eats away our will to control the mind. What then is the solution of this inner problem?

To be sure, ascetic denial is not the answer for the vast majority. Neither is the answer indulgence. The answer is in gradually educating our pleasure-urge, and in understanding the dimensions of our own being and how to harness the pleasure-urge for the purpose of self-fulfilment. This will need some elaboration.

Incidentally it is as well to make it clear that we are now discussing a general problem that faces beginners who are worldly in their dispositions. For those who are advanced aspirants some of the points we are going to discuss will not hold good. They will know what these points are; for example, the enjoyment of legitimate sense-pleasure is permissible for the ordinary person who has yet to make a start in spiritual life, but not for the person who has taken several steps in it.

'Don't seek pleasure' is hardly a practical precept for any one who has a pronounced craving for pleasure in his nature. The illumined teachers of India, besides being knowers of truth, were masters of human psychology and compassionate preceptors. What they taught on this subject can be put in a few words: seek pleasure, but in a way which will not spoil your physical or mental health, or obstruct your higher development. If you must seek physical pleasure, seek them in such a way that your powers may be preserved for enjoying the joys of the mind; seek the joys of the mind in such a way that your powers may be preserved for attaining the bliss of the spirit. Do not seek pleasure in a way that will destroy you. This should make sense to thinking people. Ethical principles, the observance of which is helpful in controlling the mind, are all meant to protect a man from harming himself. Thus they serve his profoundest interest.

The wild pleasure-urge has first to be domesticated in the frame of the requirements of self-development before it can be ready for graduation. What do we mean by 'graduation' here? Sri Ramakrishna teaches:

> ...There are three kinds of *ānanda*, joy: the joy of worldly enjoyment (*viṣayānanda*), the joy of worship (*bhajanānanda*) and the joy of Brahman (*Brahmānanda*). The joy of worldly enjoyment is the joy of sense-objects which people always enjoy. The joy of worship one enjoys while chanting the name and glories of God. And the joy of Brahman is the joy of God-vision. After experiencing the joy of God-vision the *ṛṣis* of olden times went beyond all rules and conventions.[7]

By graduation we mean passing from one of the above kinds or levels of joy to one above. We must remember that the joy of Brahman is attainable by man not only theoretically but actually. A firm faith in this truth is necessary for graduation in pleasure-seeking.

Seek sense-pleasure (*viṣayānanda*), if you must, then, but in a way which does not run counter to

---

[7]'M', op. cit., p. 404.

gaining the joy of worship (*bhajanānanda*). This can be done through developing the habit of discrimination and being discriminating in the sense-pleasures you seek. Śrī Kṛṣṇa teaches in the *Gītā*,[8] and experience corroborates, that all contact-born happiness is productive of misery. To remember this even while enjoying sense-pleasures will develop the habit of discrimination. Then it will be easier for a person to seek sense-pleasure within the frame of moral disciplines, which is meant to preserve him for enjoying the highest bliss. Along with this he should engage in suitable forms of spiritual discipline which are conducive to the joy of worship (*bhajanānanda*). Gradually, as his mind gets more and more purified, his interest in sense-enjoyment will be less and less, and his interest in the joy of worship will increase proportionately.

A time will eventually come in the life of the person who sincerely struggles on in this way, when he faces the necessity of setting aside even the joy of worship, and becoming a firm seeker of the Supreme Spirit. It is one thing to seek the benefits of seeking God and quite a different thing to seek God for His own sake, benefit or no benefit. When the seeker has inwardly grown to the extent of seeking the Supreme Spirit for its own sake and

---

[8]V. 22.

for no other motive, then his desire for pleasure will have been sublimated, and this will be conducive to perfect control of the mind. Sri Ramakrishna teaches:

> When does the attraction of sense-pleasure die away? When one realizes the consummation of all happiness and all pleasures in God—the indivisible eternal ocean of bliss. Those who enjoy Him can find no attraction in the cheap worthless pleasures of the world.
>
> He who has once tasted the refined crystal of sugar-candy finds no pleasure in tasting dirty treacle. He who has slept in a palace will not find pleasure in lying down in a hovel. The soul that has tasted the sweetness of divine bliss finds no happiness in the vulgar pleasures of the world.[9]

Many well-meaning but misdirected aspirants struggle with their desire for pleasure in a wrong way. In their earnestness they do not hesitate even to do harm to themselves, but it is all in vain. Ultimately they are vanquished, notwithstanding their honesty of purpose and sincerity. So it is very important to avoid this pitfall in handling the problem of

---

[9] *Sayings of Sri Ramakrishna* (Chennai: Sri Ramakrishna Math, 1960), sayings 244, 245.

our inner life—the desire for pleasure. Sri Ramakrishna teaches a helpful way. On being asked when the enemies of man, such as lust, anger, etc. would be vanquished, the Master replied:

> So long as these passions are directed towards the world and its objects, they behave like enemies. But when they are directed towards God, they become the best friends of man, for they lead him to God. Lust for the things of the world must be changed into hankering for God; the anger that a man feels towards his fellow men should be turned towards God for not revealing Himself. One should deal with all the passions in the same manner. These passions cannot be eradicated but can be educated.[10]

What Sri Ramakrishna appears to mean by 'passions cannot be eradicated but can be educated' is that the passions cannot be destroyed but can be harnessed and purified. If we direct our passions to lower things we remain on a lower level; by linking them to higher objectives we rise higher. If we link them to the Supreme Spirit, by their driving force we rise to Him, and they, on the other hand, are

---

[10]Ibid., saying 426.

educated and purified and cease to be passions in the ordinary sense. After a person has experientially known that he is the Ātman and not the body-mind complex, passions cease, for passion is simply desire wrongly oriented. In other words desire can be a friend or a foe according to the direction we give it. When desire is directed towards reality it becomes the instrument of liberation and joy; when it is directed towards the unreal it becomes the instrument of bondage and misery.

Vedanta traces the pleasure-motive in man to his metaphysical root, *ānanda* or bliss, the ultimate fact of existence from which man is essentially non-different. The Upaniṣad teaches:

> That which is known as the self-creator is verily the source of joy; for one becomes happy by coming in contact with that source of joy. Who, indeed, will inhale, and who will exhale, if this Bliss be not there in the supreme space (within the heart). This one, indeed, enlivens (people).[11]
>
> Certainly all beings here are, indeed, born from Bliss (*ānanda*); having been born they remain alive by Bliss; and on departing they enter into Bliss.[12]

---

[11] *Taittirīya Upaniṣad*, II. 7.

[12] Ibid., III. 6.

The very root of man's existence being bliss, it is but natural that he should instinctively seek to feel identified with it. But when he is ignorant and is identified with body and mind, he seeks it ignorantly in the body and mind and not where it is—in the Spirit. This wrong seeking of bliss in a wrong place gives rise to our pleasure-motive and its resultant bondage.

As we have said before, bliss (*ānanda*) is not pleasure, it is beyond pleasure and pain, which can never be separated on the physical and mental plane.

It is man's essential nature that urges him to seek bliss. And after much striving and fitful seeking of it on the material and mental planes, in the limited, man ultimately discovers it within his very Self—the Ātman, which is unlimited, being identical with the Supreme Spirit.

He then realizes the truth of this teaching of the Upaniṣad: 'In the Infinite alone is bliss; there is no bliss in the finite.'[13] To come to know this fact man must learn at one stage that bliss is different from pleasure and pain and that to attain it he must control his mind and give his pleasure-motive a higher direction.

---

[13]*Chāndogya Upaniṣad*, VII. 23. 1.

5

THE NATURE OF THE MIND: HINDU VIEW

The will to control the mind is not enough. We need also to know something about the nature of the mind. This we shall briefly discuss in the light of Hindu psychology, which has long had an adequate system of disciplines for controlling the mind. Hindu psychology is considered to be a science because it has through proper investigation and verification devised methods for the absolute control of the mind, leading to the attainment of perfection or illumination. What we say here is mostly derived from Hindu psychology as it is interpreted by Swami Vivekananda in his *Complete Works*.

Mind is a finer body within this gross body. The physical body is, as it were, only the outer crust of the mind. The mind being the finer part of the body, the one affects the other. It is for this reason that physical illness often affects the mind and mental illness or tension often affects the body.

Behind the mind is the Ātman, the real Self of man. Body and mind are material; Ātman is pure Spirit. Mind is not the Ātman but distinct from the Ātman.

To use an analogy from science, the difference

between matter and mind is only in the rate of vibration. Mind at a low rate of vibration is called matter: matter at a high rate of vibration is known as mind. Both matter and mind are governed by the same laws of time, space and causation.

Matter is convertible into mind, though we may not have realized that this is so. Take for instance a person who does not eat for two weeks. What happens to him? Not only does his body become emaciated, his mind also becomes blank. If he fasts for a few days more he cannot even think. He does not even remember his name. When he begins to take food, again, strength slowly returns to his body and his memory revives. Therefore it must be that food, which is matter, becomes mind.

We read in the Upaniṣad of Uddālaka teaching his son Śvetaketu by experiment how food is converted into mind. The two chapters with other relevant teachings run thus:

> 'That, my dear, which is the subtlest part of curds rises, when they are churned, and becomes butter. In the same manner, my dear, that which is the subtlest part of the food that is eaten rises and becomes mind. The subtlest part of water that is drunk rises and becomes *prāṇa*. Thus my dear, the mind consists of food, *prāṇa* consists of water, and speech consists of fire.'

The son Śvetaketu said: 'Please, venerable sir, instruct me further.'

'So be it, my dear. A person, my dear, consists of sixteen parts. Do not eat (any food) for fifteen days, but drink as much water as you like. Since the *prāṇa* consists of water, it will not be cut off if you drink water.'

Śvetaketu did not eat (any food) for fifteen days. Then he came to his father and said: 'What, sir, shall I recite?'

His father said: 'The Ṛk, Yajus and Sāman verses.'

He replied: 'They do not occur to me, sir.' (He could not remember the Vedas.)

His father said to him: 'Just as, my dear, of a great blazing fire a single coal, the size of a firefly, may be left, which would not burn much more than that, even so, my dear, of your sixteen parts only one part is left; and therefore with that one part you do not remember the Vedas. Now go and eat and you will understand me.'

Śvetaketu ate and approached his father. Then whatever his father asked him, he showed that he knew it.

Then his father said to him: 'Just as, my dear, of a great lighted fire a single coal of the size of a firefly, if left, may be made to blaze up again by adding grass to it, and will thus

> burn much more, even so, my dear, of your sixteen parts only one part was left, and that, when strengthened by food, blazed up. With it you now remember the Vedas. Therefore, my dear, the mind consists of food, the *prāṇa* consists of water, and speech consists of fire.'
>
> After that he understood what his father said; yes, he understood it.[14]

Those who doubt this teaching are invited to fast for fifteen days living only on water and see what happens to their mind!

Essentially man is not the mind but the Self or Ātman. The Ātman is ever free, infinite and eternal. It is pure consciousness. In man the free agent is not the mind but the Self. Mind is, as it were, an instrument in the Self's hands, through which the Self apprehends and responds to the external world.

This instrument with which the Self comes in contact with the external world is itself constantly changing and vacillating. When the vacillating instrument is made motionless, it can reflect the Ātman.

Though the mind is not a free agent, its powers are simply incalculable. If man has smashed the invisible atom and released its power, if man has

---

[14]Ibid., VI. 5. 5–6.

realized the unseen Ātman and become illumined, it is through the powers of the mind that he had done these things; and so with all his other achievements in the diverse fields which fall between these two poles of attainment. In fact the mind is omnipresent. Each mind is a part of the universal mind. Each mind is connected with every other mind. Therefore each mind, wherever it may be, can be in communication with the whole world.

The Upaniṣad teaches: 'He shining all these shine. Through His radiance all these become manifest in various ways.'[15] This profound teaching is to be remembered in order to understand the Hindu view of the mind. The source of all light is Brahman, the Supreme Spirit, pure consciousness. What is known as Ātman, the knowing Self of the living being, is identical with Brahman, pure consciousness. It is the radiance of this pure consciousness which manifests all things at all times.

The mind, composed of subtle matter, transparent and closest to the Self, is the inner instrument (*antaḥkaraṇa*) of this knowing Self. It is not the source of light. There is no consciousness inherent in the mind. The mind receives the radiance of consciousness from the knowing Self, whose inner instrument it is, and illuminates all things including

---

[15]*Kaṭha*, II.2.15.

physical light. Though having no light of its own the mind appears to be luminous. Though it seems to cognize, the mind is not the cognizer, but only an instrument of cognition. Shining as it does with the borrowed light of consciousness, the mind is an effective instrument of knowledge.

From our own experience we can know in a number of ways that there is a mind distinct from the organs and the body. We can think, feel, will, imagine, remember, rejoice, regret without using any of our ten organs, which proves that there is a distinct inner instrument making all these functions possible.

In order to convince those who doubt whether the mind is a distinct inner instrument the Upaniṣad gives the following argument:

> They say, 'I was absent-minded, I did not see it'; 'I was absent-minded, I did not hear it.' It is through the mind that one sees and hears. Desire, resolve, doubt, faith, want of faith, steadiness, unsteadiness, shame, intelligence and fear—all these are but the mind. Even if one is touched from behind, one knows it through the mind; therefore (the mind exists).[16]

---

[16]*Bṛhadāraṇyaka Upaniṣad,* 1.5.3.

The mind has the power of looking back into itself. With the help of the mind we can analyse the mind, and see what is going on in the mind.

According to the Hindu analysis the mind has three constituents, three levels, four functions, and five conditions, which we shall explain very briefly.

Why is it that the mind is not always found in a uniform state? The reason is that the mind is compound of three substantive forces called *guṇas*, viz. *sattva*, *rajas* and *tamas*. These *guṇas* are also the basic constituents of the entire universe, physical and mental. *Sattva* is the principle of poise conducive to purity, knowledge and joy. *Rajas* is the principle of motivity, leading to activity, desire, and restlessness. *Tamas* is the principle of inertia resulting in inaction, dullness and delusion. *Tamas* causes the mind to move on a low level; *rajas* scatters the mind and makes it restless and *sattva* gives it a higher direction.

It is not easy to define the *guṇas*. Hence Vidyāraṇya defines them according to their effects:

> Non-attachment, forgiveness, generosity, etc. are products of *sattva*. Desire, anger, avarice, etc. are products of *rajas*. Lethargy, confusion, drowsiness, etc. are products of *tamas*. When *sattva* functions in the mind merit is acquired; when *rajas* functions, demerit is produced. When *tamas* functions, neither

merit nor demerit is produced, but life is wasted for nothing.[17]

The constitution of individual minds is determined by the various combinations and permutations of these *guṇas*. This explains the varieties in human nature and also the vacillating nature of the mind.

We often say: 'I have changed my mind.' This would be impossible if the mind were composed of one substantive force only. In that case men could neither fall nor rise. All would then remain as they were born.

We are familiar with the words, conscious and subconscious. These indicate different planes on which the mind operates. On the conscious plane all work is normally accompanied by the feeling of egoism. On the subconscious plane the feeling of egoism is absent.

There is a still higher plane on which the mind can work. It can go beyond relative consciousness. Just as the subconscious is beneath consciousness, so there is another plane which is above relative consciousness. This is called the superconscious plane. Here also the feeling of egoism is absent, but there is a vast difference between this and the subconscious plane. When the mind passes beyond

---

[17] *Pañcadaśī*, II. 14–16.

the plane of relative consciousness it enters into *samādhi* or superconsciousness.

The superconscious plane of the mind is the mind in its pure state. In a sense it is then identical with Ātman. This is why Sri Ramakrishna says: 'That which is pure mind is also pure *buddhi*; that again is pure Ātman.'[18]

These three planes of conscious, subconscious and superconscious all belong to the same mind. There are not three minds in one man but three levels on which the mind operates.

The question of controlling the mind relates only to the conscious plane, where the mind is normally accompanied by the feeling of egoism. We cannot directly control the subconscious mind unless we are established in Yoga. The question of controlling the mind on the superconscious plane does not arise. But the superconscious plane can be reached only by those who have controlled their minds on the conscious and subconscious planes.

The mind in its functional aspect has four faculties, viz. *manas, buddhi, ahaṁkāra* and *citta*. *Manas* is that modification of the internal instrument (*antaḥkaraṇa*) which considers the pros and cons of a subject. *Buddhi* is that modification of the internal instrument which determines. *Citta* is that

---

[18] 'M', op. cit., p. 111.

modification of the inner instrument which remembers. *Ahaṁkāra* is that modification of the inner instrument which is characterized by self-consciousness. In every external perception these four functions of the mind are involved. These four functions follow one another so rapidly that they seem instantaneous.

The mind manifests itself in the following five conditions: 'scattering, darkening, gathering, one-pointed and concentrated.' As Swami Vivekananda explains:

> The scattering form is activity. Its tendency is to manifest in the form of pleasure or of pain. The darkening form is dullness which tends to injury.... The commentator says, the third form is natural to *devas* and angels, and the first and second to the demons. The gathering form is when it struggles to centre itself. The one-pointed form is when it tries to concentrate, and the concentrated form is what brings us to *samādhi*.[19]

The ordinary conditions of the mind are 'darkened' and 'scattered'. In the darkened state a man feels dull and passive. In the scattered state he

---

[19]*The Complete Works of Swami Vivekananda* (Calcutta: Advaita Ashrama, 1965), Vol. I, p. 243.

feels restless. Through practising the disciplines of Yoga the same mind can be 'gathered' and made 'one-pointed'. The whole purpose of mind-control is to make the mind one-pointed. When such a mind is applied to any sphere of activity, in that it shines. A businessman with a one-pointed mind will prosper in business; a musician with a one-pointed mind will become a great musician; a scientist with a one-pointed mind will become a celebrated scientist. Through the practice and development of one-pointedness, the mind reaches the fifth or highest condition, called 'concentrated'. In this condition superconsciousness is attained.

6

HOW NOT TO MAKE MIND-CONTROL UNNECESSARILY DIFFICULT

We have said something about the nature of the mind as understood in Hinduism. While this knowledge may be helpful, it will not necessarily lead to control of the mind. Much knowledge about human psychology can very well go with marked non-control of the mind. The main thing is to have a strong will to control the mind. If we have that, knowledge of psychology will certainly help, provided we steadily practise the prescribed disciplines.

By certain actions, dispositions, and habits of thought we make our task of controlling the mind almost impossible. It will be helpful to know what these are, so that we may avoid them.

If we have strong likes and dislikes, attachments and aversions, we shall not be able to control our minds.

If we live an immoral life we shall not be able to control our minds.

If we have the habit of deliberately harming others we shall not be able to control our minds.

If we indulge in intoxicants, live unbalanced and chaotic lives, e.g. eat, drink, talk, work, or sleep too little or too much, we shall not be able to control our minds.

If we habitually indulge in vain controversy, are inordinately inquisitive about others' affairs, or are too anxious to find others' faults, we shall not be able to control our minds.

If we torture our bodies unnecessarily, spend our energies in futile pursuits, force rigid silence upon ourselves, or become too egocentric, we shall not easily control our minds.

If we are over-ambitious irrespective of our capacities, if we are jealous of others' prosperity, or if we are self-righteous, we shall not easily control our minds.

If we have a feeling of guilt, we shall not be able to control our minds. Therefore we must erase all guilt from within us. To repent for sins committed and ask God's help for strength of will so that they may not be repeated, that is all that is needed to be free from guilt.

To succeed in controlling the mind one must have, in addition to strong will, faith in oneself. Śrī Kṛṣṇa says in the *Gītā*[20] that one must oneself subdue one's weakness and raise oneself by oneself. This teaching must be practised by one who intends to control his mind.

The mind will have to be controlled by the mind itself. The difficulties which we experience in controlling the mind are created by our own mind. Mind cannot be controlled by artificial means for any length of time. Deliberate, patient, intelligent, systematic hard work according to tested and suitable disciplines is needed.

7

A CLEAR GRASP OF THE TASK ON HAND NEEDED

It must be clearly understood and fully accepted that there is no gimmick by which the mind

---

[20] VI. 5.

can be controlled. Those who are in a hurry and looking for clever devices may well be warned that the mind, a delicate instrument, should be handled very carefully. The entire work of controlling the mind will have to be done by ourselves. No one else can do it for us. We cannot get it done by someone else for a fee. It is our personal task. We must do it ourselves. And we shall need great patience to do it. Swami Vivekananda teaches:

> The mind has to be gradually and systematically brought under control. The will has to be strengthened by slow, continuous, and persevering drill. This is no child's play, no fad to be tried one day and discarded the next. It is a life's work; and the end to be attained is well worth all that it can cost us to reach it; being nothing less than the realization of our absolute oneness with the Divine. Surely, with this end in view, and with the knowledge that we can certainly succeed, no price can be too great to pay.[21]

---

[21]Op. cit. (1964), Vol. V, p. 294.

8

A FAVOURABLE INNER CLIMATE NEEDS TO BE CREATED

To be able to practise the disciplines leading to the control of the mind we need to create a favourable inner climate by consciously accepting certain inevitables of life. Though they are inevitable, often enough we do not accept them as such with the result that unnecessary mental problems are created. But those who want to control their minds must scrupulously avoid loading the mind with unnecessary problems, for there are quite enough of necessary and unavoidable ones. We shall all do well to practise these teachings of the Buddha in the *Anguttara Nikāya*:

> Bhikkhus, these five things must be contemplated by all men and women, householders as well as bhikkhus.
>
> 1. Old age will come upon me some day and I cannot avoid it.
> 2. Disease can come upon me some day and I cannot avoid it.
> 3. Death will come upon me some day and I cannot avoid it.
> 4. All things that I hold dear are subject to

change and decay and separation, and I cannot avoid it.

5. I am the outcome of my own deed and whatever be my deeds, good or bad, I shall be heir to them.

Bhikkhus, by contemplating old age the pride of youth can be curbed, or at least reduced; by contemplating disease the pride of health can be curbed, or at least reduced; by contemplating death the pride of life is curbed, or at least reduced; by contemplating the change and separation of all things dear, the passionate desire for possession is curbed, or at least reduced; and by contemplating that one is the result of one's own deeds, the evil propensities of thought, word and deed are curbed, or at least reduced.

One who contemplates these five things can curb, or at least reduce, his pride and passion and thus be able to tread the path of Nirvana.[22]

The practice of these teachings of the Buddha will indirectly help purification of the mind.

---

[22]Sudhakar Dikshit, *Sermons and Sayings of the Buddha* (Mumbai: Chetana), pp. 49–50.

9

TWO SETS OF INNER DISCIPLINES

To control the mind we have to develop for ourselves two sets of inner disciplines:

a. One set is for permanent basic operation.
b. The other set is for providing high-power emergency brakes.

The first set will give a general healthy direction to the mind. The second will save us in emergencies.

If the first set is not practised, we cannot make use of the second set at all, for the simple reason that the power-supply for the second system comes from the first set of disciplines when these are effectively practised.

In the first set several basic disciplines are included:

1. Life must be held in a proper frame of constructive thinking. There should be a routine for daily life and certain basic principles by which a sense of direction is given to whatever we do. There should also be certain moral commitments by which conduct should be guided.

Those who have no moral and other principles, and no regularity of life, will find it almost impossible to control the mind. We have to bring rhythm into our life in order to control the mind.

2. To control the mind we must check its proverbial restlessness. In *Rāja-Yoga* Swami Vivekananda describes the restlessness of the mind:

'How hard it is to control the mind! Well has it been compared to the maddened monkey. There was a monkey, restless by his own nature, as all monkeys are. As if that were not enough some one made him drink freely of wine, so that he became still more restless. Then a scorpion stung him. When a man is stung by a scorpion he jumps about for a whole day; so the poor monkey found his condition worse than ever. To complete his misery a demon entered into him. What language can describe the uncontrollable restlessness of the monkey? The human mind is like that monkey, incessantly active by its own nature; then it becomes drunk with the wine of desire, thus increasing its turbulence. After desire takes possession comes the sting of the scorpion of jealousy of the success of others, and last of all the demon of pride enters the mind, making it think itself of all importance. How hard to control such a mind!'[23]

---

[23]Op. Cit. (1962), Vol. I, p. 174.

To check its restlessness we must know the causes. What are these causes? The causes of restlessness are the impurities of the mind.

10

THE PURER THE MIND THE EASIER TO CONTROL

Swami Vivekananda teaches:

> The purer the mind, the easier it is to control. Purity of the mind must be insisted upon if you would control it.... Perfect morality is the all in all of complete control over mind. The man who is perfectly moral has nothing more to do; he is free.[24]

The control of the mind depends on its purity. We are unable to control our mind because at present it is impure. If we live in a way which makes the mind more impure, and at the same time make assiduous efforts to control the mind, this will be futile. Again, if without doing anything regarding purification of the mind, we just go ahead to control our mind, we are not likely to succeed, except in the rare case when we

[24]Ibid. (1963), Vol. VI, p. 126.

start with a highly pure mind. What we need is a system of discipline for controlling the mind which will also obliterate its impurities.

What are these impurities of the mind? They are the urges, impulses and emotions like envy, hatred, anger, fear, jealousy, lust, greed, conceit, temptation, etc. born of the two lower *guṇas*, *rajas* and *tamas*. These impurities cause disturbance in the mind by creating attachment and aversion, and thus rob it of tranquillity.

How do we remove these impurities?

11

CHANGING THE CONSTITUTION OF THE MIND

The impurities of the mind can be gradually removed by providing the mind with wholesome food, and by bringing about a change in the constitution of the mind so that *sattva* predominates over the other two *guṇas*. Finally, it is true, *sattva* has to be transcended; but first it has to predominate.

We mentioned earlier that according to the teachings of the Upaniṣad the mind consists of food.[25] In elaborating this teaching the Upaniṣad says:

---

[25]*Chāndogya Upaniṣad*, VI. 5.4.

> The food that we eat is transformed in three different ways: the grossest part of it becomes excrement, the middle part is transformed into flesh, and the subtlest part goes to form the mind.[26]

Further:

> Just as in the churning of curds, the subtlest part rises up and is transformed into butter, so when food is eaten, the subtlest part rises up and is transformed into mind.[27]

As the mind consists of food, naturally the teaching follows:

> When the food is pure, the mind becomes pure. When the mind becomes pure, memory becomes firm. And when a man is in possession of firm memory, all the bonds which tie him down to the world are loosed.[28]

According to the commentary of Śaṅkarācārya the word 'food' in the text means anything that is taken in by the senses, that is to say, sounds, sights,

---

[26]Ibid., VI. 5.1.
[27]Ibid., VI. 6.1–2.
[28]Ibid., VII. 26.2.

smells, etc. And 'the mind becomes pure' means that it becomes free from aversion, attachment or delusion, which create disquiet in the mind, making it difficult to control. So one of the basic methods of controlling the mind is to desist from taking such 'food' as will cause attachment, aversion and delusion.

But how do we know which food will cause attachment, aversion and delusion? Broadly speaking, according to the *Gītā*, *rājasika* and *tāmasika* food cause attachment, aversion and delusion. *Sāttvika* food helps a person to reduce attachment, aversion and delusion. It is not only what is usually taken through the mouth for nourishment which will have something to do with the state of the mind. Liquor and drugs are also taken through the mouth, and they also affect the mind. We can easily see the difference in effect when we drink a glass of sugar-candy water and a glass of liquor. The effect of drugs on the state of the mind is well known. Also, as we have noted, what we see with our eyes, hear with our ears, and what we touch, have great effect on our minds. A movie, or an oration, can set in motion waves of various sorts in the mind, making it difficult or easy to control.

So, in moulding the conditions favourable for controlling the mind, judicious eating and drinking are of some help. Equally important is the intake through the other senses. In the choice of food, persons desiring to control the mind will do well to prefer *sāttvika* to *rājasika* and *tāmasika* foods. So far as food taken through the mouth is concerned, the *Gītā* is our best guide:

> The foods which augment vitality, energy, strength, health, cheerfulness and appetite, which are savoury and oleaginous, substantial and agreeable, are liked by the *sāttvika*.
>
> The foods that are bitter, sour, saline, excessively hot, pungent, dry and burning are liked by the *rājasika* and are productive of pain, grief and disease.
>
> That which is stale and tasteless, stinking, cooked overnight, refuse and impure is the food liked by the *tāmasika*.[29]

What is liked by *sāttvika*, *rājasika* and *tāmasika* persons is also conducive to developing *sāttvika*, *rājasika* and *tāmasika* minds respectively.

Human nature being constituted by varying combinations of the three substantive forces, *sattva*, *rajas* and *tamas*, the predominance of one of the three *guṇas* over the other two determines the dominant tone of a man's nature. A man with a preponderance of *rajas* or *tamas* in his nature

---

[29] XVII. 8–10.

cannot behave, in spite of himself, like a man with a preponderance of *sattva*. This is why Śrī Kṛṣṇa says in despair, as it were, in the *Gītā*: 'Even a wise man acts in accordance with his own nature: beings follow nature: what can restraint do?'[30]

If restraint can do nothing, if human nature is predetermined and incapable of being changed, then there is little sense in discussing how to control the mind. The implication of this statement of the Lord, therefore, seems to be: man must change his nature, physical and mental, in order to be able to control the mind. So long as *rajas* or *tamas* predominates in the constitution of our mind, we cannot control it, however much we may try. The reason for this should be understood. According to the teachings of Vedanta:

> *Rajas* has its *vikṣepa-śakti* or projecting power, which is of the nature of an activity, and from which this primeval flow of activity has emanated. From this also, mental modifications such as attachment and grief are continually produced.
>
> Lust, anger, avarice, arrogance, spite, egoism, envy, jealousy etc.—these are the dire attributes of *rajas*, from which the worldly

---

[30] Ibid., III. 33.

> tendency of man is produced. Therefore *rajas* is a cause of bondage.
>
> *Āvṛti* or the veiling power is the power of *tamas*, which makes things appear other than which they are. It is this that causes man's repeated transmigrations, and starts the action of the projecting power.
>
> Absence of right judgement, or contrary judgement, want of definite belief and doubt—these certainly never desert one who has any connection with this veiling power, and then the projecting power gives ceaseless trouble.[31]

The psychological consequences of the predominance of the projecting power of *rajas* and the veiling power of *tamas* make controlling the mind in which these powers are dominant a difficult task. Yet there is another constituent of the mind which makes the task not a hopeless one. The constituent is *sattva*, which is found in a mixed or pure state. On this, Vedanta teaches:

> Pure *sattva* is (clear) like water, yet in conjunction with *rajas* and *tamas*, it makes for

---

[31]Śrī Śaṅkarācārya, *Vivekacūḍāmaṇi*, tr. by Swami Madhavananda (Calcutta: Advaita Ashrama), verses 111—13, 115.

transmigration. The reality of Ātman becomes reflected in *sattva*, and like the sun reveals the entire world of matter. The traits of mixed *sattva* are an utter absence of pride etc., *niyama, yama*, etc., as well as faith, devotion, yearning for liberation, the divine tendencies, and turning away from the unreal.

The traits of pure *sattva* are cheerfulness, the realization of one's own Self, supreme peace, contentment, bliss, and steady devotion to Ātman by which the aspirant enjoys bliss everlasting.[32]

So we find—and it is very important to understand this—that built into our own nature are powerful impediments and potent help in controlling the mind. It is therefore a question of devising the right strategy so that the inimical forces may be defeated and the helpful forces given full play. This can be done not by engaging in a blind mad fight, but by skilfully operating the inner forces.

The strategic question in regard to the control of mind is this: can we so change the *guṇa*-balance in our nature as to bring about the preponderance of *sattva*? Teachings on this problem are therefore of great help to us. In the *Śrīmad Bhāgavatam* we find:

---

[32]Ibid., 117–19.

The *guṇas, sattva, rajas* and *tamas,* belong to the intellect and not to the Self. Through *sattva* one should subdue the other two and subdue *sattva* also by means of *sattva* itself.

Through developed sattva a man attains that form of spirituality which consists in devotion to Me. Through the use of *sāttvika* things (i.e. those that tends to purity and illumination and so on) *sattva* is developed; this leads to spirituality.

That superior form of spirituality which is brought on by an increase of *sattva* destroys *rajas* and *tamas.* And when both of them are destroyed, iniquity which has its rise in them, is also quickly destroyed.[33]

In the teaching that through developed *sattva* the aspirant attains spirituality we get the most important lesson for our purpose, for attainment of spirituality and mind-control are identical in one sense. So, of utmost importance for those who want to control the mind is to know how to develop *sattva.*

What are the *sāttvika* things and activities by means of which *sattva* can be made to predominate? Śri Kṛṣṇa specifies them in the next verse:

---

[33]Book XI, chapter 13, verses 1–3.

> Scriptures, water, people, place, time, work, birth, meditation, *mantra*, and purification—these are the ten causes which develop the *guṇas*.[34]

The import of this verse is that each of these has its *sāttvika, rājasika* and *tāmasika* counterparts; the first conducing to purity, illumination, and bliss; the second to temporary pleasure followed by painful reaction; and the last leading to ignorance and increasing bondage. The teaching continues:

> Of these, those alone are *sāttvika*, which the sages praise; the *tāmasa* are what they condemn; while those are *rājasa* about which they are indifferent.
>
> For the increase of *sattva* a man should concern himself with *sāttvika* things alone. Thence comes spirituality, and from this again knowledge, leading to the realization of one's independence and the removal of the superimposition of gross and subtle bodies.[35]

The import of the last verse is:

> Only those scriptures are to be followed

---

[34]Ibid., verse 4.

[35]Ibid., verses 5, 6.

which teach *nivṛtti* or the march back to the oneness of Brahman, not those that teach *pravṛtti* or continuing the multiplicity (*rājasika*) or those that teach downright injurious tenets (*tāmasika*). Similarly holy water only is to be used, not scented water or wine, etc.; one should mix only with spiritual people, not with worldly-minded or wicked people. A solitary place is to be preferred, not a public thoroughfare or a gaming-house. Early morning or some such time is to be selected for meditation in preference to hours likely to cause distraction or dullness. Obligatory and unselfish works alone should be done, not selfish or harmful ones. Initiation into pure and non-injurious forms of religion is needed, not those that require much ado or those that are impure and harmful. Meditation should be on the Lord, not on sense-objects or on enemies with a view to revenge. *Mantras* such as *Om* are to be preferred, not those bringing worldly prosperity or causing injury to others. Purification of the mind is what we should be interested in, not merely trimming up the body or cleaning up houses.[36]

---

[36]Ibid., verse 6, Śrīdhara's gloss.

In the verses quoted above we have, from an authentic source, all-important teachings on how to bring about desirable transformation in the *guṇa*-combination in our mind. Control of mind, in its creative and positive aspect, is this inner transformation. Until this is achieved no true work is really done for gaining control over the mind.

When through these and other means the aspirant has succeeded in ensuring the preponderance of *sattva* in his nature, his battle for mind-control is more than half won, but not fully. The reason is that even *sattva* binds man. This is how the *Gītā* puts it:

> *Sattva, rajas* and *tamas*—these *guṇas*, O mighty-armed, born of Prakṛti, bind fast in the body the indestructible embodied one.
>
> Of these *sattva*, because of its stainlessness, luminous and free from evil, binds, O sinless one, by attachment to happiness and by attachment to knowledge.[37]

Sri Ramakrishna in his parable of the man and the three robbers, explains the matter as follows:

> This world itself is the forest. The three

[37]XIV. 5, 6.

robbers prowling here are *sattva, rajas* and *tamas*. It is they that rob a man of the knowledge of Truth. *Tamas* wants to destroy him. *Rajas* binds him to the world. But *sattva* rescues him from the clutches of *rajas* and *tamas*. Under the protection of *sattva*, man is rescued from anger, passion, and other evil effects of *tamas*. Further, *sattva* loosens the bonds of the world. But *sattva* also is a robber. It cannot give him the ultimate knowledge of Truth, though it shows him the road leading to the supreme abode of God. Setting him on the path, *sattva* tells him: 'Look yonder. There is your home.' Even *sattva* is far away from the knowledge of Brahman.[38]

The psychological implication of the words of the *Gītā* that '*sattva* binds by attachment to happiness and attachment to knowledge', and of Sri Ramakrishna, that '*sattva* is also a robber', is that even the preponderance of *sattva* in our nature does not amount to perfect control of the mind. What is needed for gaining perfect control of the mind is to go beyond the *guṇas*. Śrī Kṛṣṇa teaches the technique of going beyond the *guṇas* in the fourteenth chapter of the *Gītā*. In verse twenty-six

---

[38] 'M', op. cit., pp. 207–08.

he gives the entire teaching in its simplest form, shorn of all technicalities. He says: 'And he who serves Me (the Lord) with unswerving devotion, he, going beyond the *guṇas*, is fitted for becoming Brahman.'

But only the pure in heart can serve God with unswerving devotion. If we feel that we are not so pure in heart and so cannot practise unswerving devotion, we must not be discouraged. Through the persistent practice of devotion we can gradually become more unswerving and pure.

However, if for any reason we are not able to adopt the 'simplest method' of going beyond the *guṇas*, other ways of controlling the mind remain open to us.

In addition to learning how to conquer *tamas* and *rajas* we need to learn how to conquer *sattva* also. This is taught by Śrī Śaṅkarācārya thus:

> *Tamas* is destroyed by both *sattva* and *rajas*, *rajas* by *sattva*, and *sattva* dies when purified. Therefore do away with thy superimposition through the help of *sattva*.[39]

---

[39] *Vivekacūḍāmaṇi*, 278.

12

HOLY COMPANY GREATLY HELPS MIND-CONTROL

We have discussed in some detail one method of changing the *guṇa*-composition of our mind for the purpose of controlling it. This is an authentic method taught in the scriptures. When correctly practised it can help any one.

There will, however, be many people who are so constituted that they cannot take inner care of themselves in such detail, or because their conditions of living are not conducive to the practice of this discipline. Is there any other discipline easier to practise but equally effective? Yes, there is a discipline which is easier to practise, and is equally, if not more effective.

But there is a difficulty in speaking about this very simple method. An illustration will show what we mean. There are some patients who, having suffered a great deal from an obstinate ailment, do not really trust the doctor when he prescribes a simple remedy. They are inclined to think that a difficult disease needs correspondingly complicated treatment. The same is true of the simple method we are about to describe: for some people it is too simple.

The method is that of being in holy company.

It is a simple method, but more effective than all others. Śrī Kṛṣṇa teaches:

> Yoga, discrimination, piety, study of the Vedas, austerities, renunciation, rites such as *agnihotra*, works of public utility, charity, vows, sacrifices, secret *mantras*, places of pilgrimage, and moral rules, particular as well as universal—none of these, I say, bind Me so much as association with saints, which roots out all attachment.[40]

Most of our attachments are due to the preponderance of *rajas* in our nature. When we are in the company of a perfected soul, the powerful vibrations of his holiness penetrate within us and bring about a speedy change in the *guṇa*-composition of our mind, leading to a preponderance of *sattva* for the time being. How enduring this *sattva*-dominance will be depends on how often we frequent holy company. Sri Ramakrishna teaches:

> ...The worldly man must constantly live in the company of holy men. It is necessary for all, even for *sannyāsins;* but it is specially necessary for the householder. His disease has

---

[40] *Śrīmad Bhāgavatam*, XI. 12. 1, 2.

become chronic because he has to live constantly in the midst of 'woman and gold'.[41]

Holy company makes our task of controlling the mind easier, so we must not fail to seek it. But when holy company is not available, what do we do? We must depend on our own resources and go ahead with hard and methodical work. Following those of the above teachings which are suitable for us, we must bring about the preponderance of *sattva* in our mind, and finally learn how to transcend *sattva* by purifying it.

13

HOW IS SATTVA PURIFIED

According to Vedanta, the purification of *sattva* takes place through constant discrimination between the real and the unreal, through renunciation of the unreal, and through deep contemplation on the true nature of the Self. In this connection what Śaṅkarācārya teaches by implication on mind-control is helpful:

The desire of Self-realization is obscured

---

[41] 'M', op. cit., p. 269.

> by innumerable desires for things other than the Self. When they have been destroyed by constant attachment to the Self, the Ātman clearly manifests Itself of Its own accord.
>
> As the mind becomes gradually established in the inmost Self, it proportionately gives up desires for external objects. And when all such desires have been eliminated, there takes place the unobstructed realization of the Ātman.
>
> The yogi's mind dies, being constantly fixed on his own Self. Thence follows the cessation of desires. Therefore do away with your superimposition.[42]

This 'death' of the mind does not mean loss of the mind, but perfect purification, in which state it is identified with the Ātman. When one knows oneself as the Ātman, there is no longer a mind needing control.

In seeking to control of our mind we must aspire to this absolute state of being. As long as we have more desires than one, or other desires than the desire for the realization of Ātman, it will be difficult to control the mind, for it will then be in a scattered state. If we seek anything less than the

---

[42] Op. cit., 275–77.

highest, into which everything converges, as it were, the mind will be divided. It is hard to control a divided mind. In other words, those who seek anything less than perfect illumination, or realization of the Self, can never control their mind perfectly. They have some desire other than that for illumination and therefore they in effect vote for the perpetuation of *avidyā*. Thus they render themselves incapable of doing things needed for controlling the mind. In Vedanta, mind in its impure state is identified with *avidyā*.[43] And so the disciplines that are enjoined for the removal of *avidyā* are also applicable to mind-control. Of these disciplines one particularly is very helpful in controlling the mind through its power of purification. This discipline, in Vedantic terminology, is *svādhyāsāpanayam*, doing away with the superimposition that has come upon oneself, or in other words, conquering the identification with the non-Self.

About superimposition on the Self and the method of its removal Śaṅkarācārya teaches:

> The idea of 'me and mine' in the body, organs, etc., which are the non-Self—this superimposition the wise man must put a stop to, by identifying himself with the Ātman.

---

[43]Ibid., 169, 180.

> Realizing your inmost Self, the witness of the *buddhi* (intellect) and its modifications, and constantly revolving the positive thought 'I am That', conquer the identification with the non-Self.[44]

All the disquiet, tension, and problems of the mind have only one origin, the false identification of one's real Self with the non-Self, giving rise to the idea of 'me and mine' in the body, the organs, etc.[45] The cure of all these disorders is in the effective practice of the positive thought 'I am That', 'I am the Ātman.' The Reality-oriented mind alone can be controlled.

The practice of *sādhana-catustaya*, the fourfold Vedantic disciplines,[46] which is enjoined for the

---

[44]Ibid., 268–69.

[45]Śaṅkarācārya says in *Vivekacūḍāmaṇi* (311): 'He alone who has identified himself with the body is greedy after sense-pleasures. How can one devoid of the body-idea be greedy (like him)?'

Cf. Swami Vivekananda, op. cit. (1963), Vol. VI, p. 124: 'There is but one way to control the senses—to see Him who is the Reality in the universe. Then and then alone can we really conquer our senses.'

[46]The fourfold Vedantic discipline is:

i Discrimination between things permanent and transient.

attainment of illumination, takes care of the problem of mind-control as a matter of course.

These Vedantic disciplines for controlling the mind can be helpfully supplemented by certain yoga disciplines which we shall now discuss.

14

BASIC YOGA DISCIPLINES FOR MIND-CONTROL

Basic yoga scriptures insist that in order to control the mind aspirants must practise the disciplines of *yama* and *niyama*. Non-killing, truthfulness, non-stealing, continence, and non-receiving of gifts are called *yamas*.[47] Internal and external purification, contentment, mortification, study, and worship of God are the *niyamas*.[48]

---

ii Renunciation of the enjoyment of the fruits of action in this world and hereafter.

iii The cultivation of six treasures: restraining the outgoing mental propensities; restraining the external sense-organs; withdrawing the self; forbearance; self-settledness; and faith.

iv Longing for liberation.

(Sadānanda, *Vedāntasāra*, 15.)

[47]*Yoga-sūtra* of Patañjali, II. 30.

[48]Ibid., 32.

Obviously one who is not yet the master of his mind will fail to observe some of these precepts. Yet the idea of insisting on the practice of these virtues is to keep the ideal always bright before the practitioner, so that inner strength may grow through self-effort. Patañjali, the great teacher of yoga, says:

Undisturbed calmness of mind is attained by cultivating:

a. Friendliness towards the happy.
b. Compassion for the unhappy.
c. Delight in the good.
d. Indifference to the evil.[49]

This aphorism requires explanation. The disposition of being happy at the happiness of others creates a very soothing mental climate in which wrong impulses like jealousy cannot thrive.

Contraction of the heart causes us a special type of inner disquiet, and this can be removed only through the expansion of our heart. Practising compassion for the unhappy is one of the methods of doing this. Active compassion will mean service to the afflicted. Service done in the proper attitude is purifying. It expands our hearts, enhances our

---

[49]Ibid., 33.

sense of identity with the whole, and liberates us from the cramping agony of our smallness. This gives us inner joy.

Even if we ourselves are miserable, there will be no dearth of more miserable persons around us. Let us do something for somebody else. If we cannot do anything else, we may just be friendly and pray sincerely for the good of the world. That too will help.

Our delight should be in the good. When we take delight in the good the psychological law is that we imbibe the goodness and the other qualities of the good. Goodness is conducive to calmness of mind.

We are asked to be indifferent to the evil. Undoubtedly to try to change evil people into good is a high and noble task. But that task is for the prophet and the saint, not for the ordinary man who is struggling with his own mind. As long as our own minds are not well under control, we should studiously avoid evil company. In that way we can save our own minds from catching the contagion and getting into greater trouble. If we feel so deeply for the evil and the wicked we can pray for their welfare. This will help both, them and us.

But who are those wicked people? Who judges who is wicked? There can be a long controversy on the issue. For all practical purposes, however, those who live immoral and unethical lives can be considered wicked people.

While avoidance of evil company is helpful for controlling the mind in the negative way, the company of the holy is helpful in the most positive manner. Holy company removes the mental impurities of even a degraded person. This is what the saints and scriptures say. Śrī Kṛṣṇa teaches in the *Śrīmad Bhāgavatam*[50] that association with the holy roots out all attachment. Our attachments are the most powerful impediments to the control of the mind. When attachments are removed, aversions and delusions also leave us easily, as a result of which we attain right discrimination and clarity of understanding. With these inner transformations unknowingly going on as a result of holy company we find it possible to control the mind.

15

PRACTICE OF DISCRIMINATION HELPS

There are situations in which we do things deliberately, knowing full well that it is the right thing to do. And there are situations in which we act impulsively without knowing the right or wrong of them. But in either case every work bears

[50]I. 12.1 and 26.26.

its own fruits, sweet or bitter. Apart from other sufferings one result of wrong action is greater mental turmoil. Our ignorance about right and wrong will not save us from trouble.

Therefore in order to control the mind one essential thing is to learn how to discriminate between right and wrong, good and evil, real and unreal. When discrimination becomes a habit with us we shall automatically ask ourselves: What good is it? This will save us from possible mental turmoil resulting from wrong, rash and foolish actions, provided we have developed the habit of doing only what our discrimination tells us to be good. The practice of discrimination may very well go hand in hand with the practice of self-examination. This conduces to self-improvement.

There is another dimension to the practice of discrimination which helps the control of the mind in a fundamental manner. The crux of the problem of mind-control was neatly put by the ancient seekers, Sanaka and others, to Brahmā in these few words:

> O Lord, the mind is attached to the sense-objects and the sense-objects influence the mind. So, for the man, who seeks liberation and wants to go beyond them, how do they cease to act and react upon each other?[51]

---

[51]Ibid., XI. 14. 17.

The crux of the problem remains the same even today. And given a universe on the same plan, it will ever remain so. The authoritative answer that came from Śrī Kṛṣṇa to this important question has been summarized in the following words:

> If the mind, which is connected with sense-objects as agent and enjoyer etc. and is variously named as intellect, egoism and so forth, were the reality of the *jīva* (living being), then there might not be a dissolution of the connection between the *jīva* and the sense-objects. But the *jīva* is eternally identified with Brahman, and his *apparent* connection with the sense-objects is due to the superimposition of the mind on him. Hence by considering oneself to be Brahman and reflecting on the unreality of the sense-objects, one should turn away from them and worship the Lord so that one can remain in one's true nature as the infinite Self.[52]

---

[52]*The Last Message of Sri Krishna*, tr. by Swami Madhavananda (Calcutta: Advaita Ashrama, 1956), pp. 118–19.

16

TRAINING THE MIND TO BEHAVE

In one sense to control the mind is to train it to *behave*. It is like catching a wild horse and turning it into a circus horse to do feats to order. How is it done?

Swami Vivekananda teaches:

> Before we can control the mind we must study it.
>
> We have to seize this unstable mind and drag it from its wanderings and fix it on one idea. Over and over again this must be done. By power of will we must get hold of the mind and make it stop and reflect upon the glory of God.
>
> The easiest way to get hold of the mind is to sit quiet and let it drift where it will for a while. Hold fast to the idea, 'I am the witness watching my mind drifting. The mind is not I.' Then see it think as if it were a thing entirely apart from yourself. Identify yourself with God, never with matter or with the mind. Picture the mind as a calm lake stretched before you and the thoughts that come and go as bubbles rising and breaking on its surface. Make no effort to control the thoughts, but

> watch them and follow them in imagination as they float away. This will gradually lessen the circles. For the mind ranges over wide circles of thought and those circles widen out into ever increasing circles, as in a pond when we throw a stone into it. We want to reverse the process and starting with a huge circle make it narrower until at last we can fix the mind on one point and make it stay there. Hold to the idea, 'I am not the mind, I see that I am thinking, I am watching my mind act', and each day the identification of yourself with thought and feeling will grow less, until at last you can entirely separate yourself from the mind and actually know it to be apart from yourself.
>
> When this is done, the mind is your servant to control as you will. The first stage of being a yogi is to go beyond the senses. When the mind is conquered, he has reached the highest stage.[53]

We shall be surprised to see, when we begin this practice, how many hideous thoughts will come to our mind. As the practice continues the turbulence of the mind may increase for some time. But the more detached from our minds we shall

[53]Op. cit. (1964), Vol. VIII, pp. 47–48.

find it possible to feel ourselves, the less will be its pranks. Gradually its vagaries will lose all vigour under the penetrating gaze of the observer, and finally the mind will become like a circus horse, vigorous but disciplined. We should for some time deliberately watch our minds every day at regular intervals. And this should continue as long as the mind needs to be taught how to behave.

17

PRACTICE OF PRĀṆĀYĀMA

We shall notice that when our mind is in a disturbed state our breathing becomes faster and irregular. One of the ways of quieting the mind is to regularize the breathing. Regular practice of deep breathing helps to develop a stable state of mind.

It may be mentioned here that the practice of *prāṇāyāma* (restraining the breath in order to get control of the *prāṇa* or vital force) is very helpful for controlling the mind. *Prāṇāyāma* should, however, be learnt directly from a teacher, and should be practised in a clean atmosphere. Besides, those who do not practise continence, or have a diseased heart, lungs or nervous system, are advised not to practise *prāṇāyāma*.

18

PRACTICE OF PRATYĀHĀRA

Usually our condition is that we are forced to concentrate our minds on certain things. There are attractions in objects which compel our minds to become fixed on them. In this way we become the slaves of tempting objects. The true position, however, should be that we put our minds on things at will. Things should not be able to force our minds on them. Learning to do this is a most important step in controlling the mind. In fact, until we learn to do this, nothing is practically achieved by way of controlling the mind.

Now, how do we do this? Swami Vivekananda teaches:

> We hear 'Be good', and 'Be good', and 'Be good', taught all over the world. There is hardly a child, born in any country in the world, who has not been told, 'Do not steal', 'Do not tell a lie', but nobody tells the child how he can help doing them. Talking will not help him. Why should he not become a thief? We do not teach him how not to steal; we simply tell him, 'Do not steal.' Only when we teach him to control his mind do we really help him. All actions, internal and external,

> occur when the mind joins itself to certain centres, called the organs. Willingly or unwillingly it is drawn to join itself to centres, and that is why people do foolish deeds and feel miserable, which, if the mind were under control, they would not do. What would be the result of controlling the mind? It then would not join itself to the centres of perception, and, naturally, feeling and willing would be under control. It is clear so far. Is it possible? It is perfectly possible.[54]

It can be done by practising the discipline of *pratyāhāra* which is taught by Patañjali.

What is *pratyāhāra*? *Pratyāhāra* is that abstention by which the senses do not come into contact with their objects and follow, as it were, the nature of the (controlled) mind.

> When the mind is withdrawn from the sense-objects the sense-organs also withdraw themselves from their objects and they are said to imitate the mind. This is known as *pratyāhāra*.[55]

The link between the sense-organs and sense-

---

[54]Ibid. (1962), Vol. I, p. 171.

[55]*Yoga-sūtra* of Patañjali, II. 54.

objects is the mind. When the mind is withdrawn from sense-objects, the sense-organs also imitate the mind, that is to say, they also withdraw themselves from their objects. When the mind is restrained, the senses are then automatically restrained. This example illustrates the point: just as the bees fly when the queen flies, and alight when the queen alights, so the senses become restrained when the mind is restrained. This is *pratyāhāra*.

The entire secret of *pratyāhāra* is will-power, which every normal person is capable of developing; but in most people it is in an undeveloped state. When confirmed in *pratyāhāra* one attains mastery over one's senses, thoughts and emotions. Practice of *pratyāhāra* helps develop will-power and will-power helps develop *pratyāhāra*.

19

IMPORTANCE OF HARMONIOUS HUMAN RELATIONS

In the Sermon on the Mount Christ says: '…If thou bring thy gift to the altar and there remember that thy brother hath ought against thee, leave there thy gift before the altar, and go thy way; first be reconciled to thy brother and then come and offer thy gift.'[56]

---

[56]Matthew, 5. 23–24.

This is an important teaching of Christ. Our human relations have much to do with our states of mind, on which depends the building up of spiritual life.

Those who want to control their minds must not store up ill-feelings or grievances or other wrong impulses in the mind, which is to be used for higher purposes. Through doing one's duties to others, and through the practice of detachment, forgiveness and humility, we must keep our human relations straight. Holy Mother says: 'Forgiveness is *tapasyā* (austerity).'[57]

A healthy mind is much easier to control than an unhealthy or broken mind. Here is a case history which will indicate how forgiveness helps in restoring the health of the mind. Years ago, Dr. Jung suggested that psychologists and clergymen should join hands in alleviating human suffering. The *American Magazine* of October 1947 published an article describing a remarkable clinic of this kind designed to mend broken souls and restore shattered faith:

> A thirty-four-year-old woman came to this clinic. She looked like a woman of fifty and had for months suffered from insomnia,

---

[57] *Sri Sarada Devi: The Holy Mother* (Chennai: Sri Ramakrishna Math, 1949), p. 457.

nervousness and chronic fatigue. She had consulted doctors, but to no avail. Religious at heart, she tried to pray but without success. She finally became so depressed that she wanted to commit suicide. The clinic psychiatrist discovered the real cause of her illness: a deep resentment towards her sister who had married the man she herself wanted to marry. Outwardly she was kind to her sister, but deep in her subconscious mind she cherished a terrible hatred which ruined her mental and physical health. Then a minister came to her aid. 'You know it is evil to hate. You must ask God to help you to forgive your sister in your heart; then God will give you peace.' She followed this advice. 'Through prayer and faith in a power greater than herself she has been able to forgive her sister. Her depression and insomnia are gone. She is a new person and happier than ever before.'[58]

[58]Swami Yatiswarananda, *Adventures in Religious Life* (Chennai: Sri Ramakrishna Math, 1959), pp. 159–60.

20

HEALTHY OCCUPATION OF THE MIND NEEDED

The common saying 'an idle brain is the devil's workshop' is very true. Therefore the mind must be given healthy and creative occupation. It should be fed with high thoughts and noble inspiration. Otherwise it will drift to low things and become scattered. In its scattered state the mind cannot be controlled.

If we can penetrate to the core of the unsteadiness of our mind, there we shall discover as its cause a wrong thought, or many wrong thoughts, one acting upon another. So, to steady the mind we need to guard our thoughts with maximum steadfastness. There are these Buddhist teachings:

> As a fletcher makes straight his arrow, a wise man makes straight his trembling and unsteady thought, which is difficult to guard, difficult to hold back.
>
> Let the wise man guard his thoughts, for they are difficult to perceive, very artful and they rush wherever they listeth; thoughts well-guarded bring happiness.
>
> If a man's thoughts are not dissipated, if

> his mind is not perplexed, if it has ceased to think of good and evil then there is no fear for him while he is watchful.[59]

Right introspection will reveal that inadvertence is at the root of much of our mental turmoil. And inadvertence comes to us so naturally because we are not trained in cultivating our mind for higher inner occupations. Śrī Śaṅkarācārya teaches:

> One should never be careless in one's steadfastness to Brahman. Bhagavān Sanatkumāra, who is Brahmā's son, has called inadvertence death itself.
>
> There is no greater danger for the *jñānin* than carelessness about his own real nature. From this comes delusion, thence egoism; this is followed by bondage, and then comes misery.
>
> Finding even a wise man hankering after sense-objects, oblivion torments him through the evil propensities of the *buddhi*, as a woman does her doting paramour.
>
> As sedge, even if removed, does not stay away for a moment, but covers the water again, so Māyā or Nescience also covers even

[59]*Dhammapada*, verses 33, 36, 39.

> a wise man, if he is averse to meditation on the Self.
>
> If the mind ever so slightly strays from the Ideal and becomes outgoing, then it goes down and down, just as a play-ball inadvertently dropped on the staircase bounds down from one step to another.[60]

Steadfast cultivation of awareness of the highest objective of life, which is the Supreme Spirit, is a potent method of steadying the mind. In fact, when we practise this discipline we shall derive greater benefit from other practices.

A healthy preoccupation of the mind need not necessarily be monotonous. If it should be, it might turn into unhealthy drudgery. There can be a chosen, refreshing variety to ensure the healthy preoccupation of the mind. Śrī Kṛṣṇa teaches:

> Charity, the performance of one's duty, the observance of vows, general and particular, the hearing of the scriptures, meritorious acts, and all other works—all these culminate in the control of the mind. The control of the mind is the highest yoga.[61]

---

[60] *Vivekacūḍāmaṇi*, verses 321–25.

[61] *Śrīmad Bhāgavatam*, XI. 23. 46.

21

IMPORTANCE OF RIGHT USE OF THE IMAGINATION

Man is endowed with the faculty of imagination. A great deal of our mental troubles and difficulties in controlling the mind arises from our habitual wrong use of this faculty. It is common practice with many of us to indulge in what is called emotional kite-flying, day-dreaming, and wild, meaningless and purposeless speculation of various sorts. Our expectations may be imaginary, without any basis in fact, but they bring us real disappointments. Our fears may be baseless, but they cause genuine trepidation in our heart. Through exercising our power of imagination we make unreal things real for ourselves. And we become victims of worries and concerns for which there is no factual basis. When this habit becomes a hardened one, it is extremely difficult to control the mind. Sometimes we may not even be aware of the fact that for a good part of our day we live in a dreamland, in a world of shadows and not in that of truth and facts.

Unless we get rid of this habit we shall find it extremely difficult to control the mind. How do we do it? The following story will give us an important clue:

A somewhat inebriated gentleman was slowly moving along the street, carrying in his hand a box with perforations on the lid and sides. It appeared he was carrying some live animal in the box. An acquaintance stopped him and asked, 'What have you got in the box?'

'It is a mongoose' replied the tipsy man.

'What on earth for?'

'Well you know how it is with me; I am not really drunk now, but soon I shall be. And when I am, I see snakes all around and I get awfully scared. That is what I have the mongoose for, to protect me from the snakes.'

'Good heavens, those are all imaginary snakes!'

'This also, is an imaginary mongoose!'

The box was in fact empty.[62]

Similarly we require one imagination to counteract another. We require a right imagination to throw out wrong ones. Swami Vivekananda teaches: 'Imagination properly employed is our greatest friend; it goes beyond reason and is the only light that takes us everywhere.'[63] The purest of imaginations is the thought of God. The more we cling to the thought of God, the less will be our trouble with the mind.

---

[62]Swami Yatiswarananda, op. cit., p. 263.

[63]Op. cit. (1964), Vol. VIII, p. 49.

22

IMPORTANCE OF MEDITATION

Meditation on God is the most effective way of controlling the mind. Meditation and control of the mind go hand in hand. The highest objective for which one controls the mind is meditationon God or Ātman as the case may be. However, meditation also helps control of the mind.

The mind must be riveted on something which is not only pure in itself but can also purify our mind through its power. Meditation on God is advised, because one becomes imbued with the quality of the object on which one meditates.

In meditation, whenever the mind strays away one should indefatigably bring it back and place it on the object of meditation. Swami Brahmananda, one of the great direct disciples of Sri Ramakrishna, says:

> Unless you meditate, the mind cannot be controlled, and unless the mind is controlled, you cannot meditate. But if you think, 'First let me control the mind and then I shall meditate', You will never enter the path of spiritual life. You must do both at the same

time—steady your mind and meditate.[64]

So, when once a disciple asked Swami Brahmananda, 'Maharaj, how can one control the mind?' the teacher, in effect, explained how the above instruction was to be put into practice. He said:

> Through gradual practice the mind has to be concentrated upon God. Keep a sharp eye on the mind so that no undesirable thoughts or distractions may enter in. Whenever they try to crowd in your mind, turn it towards God and pray earnestly. Through such practice the mind comes under control and becomes purified.[65]

23

GUARD AGAINST DESPONDENCY

These are the basic disciplines. They should be regularly practised by those who intend to control their minds. While steadfastly practising these disciplines, the aspirant's motto should be: struggle, struggle and struggle; never give in.

---

[64]Swami Prabhavananda, *The Eternal Companion: Spiritual Teachings of Swami Brahmananda* (Chennai: Sri Ramakrishna Math, 1945), p. 229.

[65]Ibid., p. 197.

We must not allow despondency to eat into our earnestness and energy. Despondency is the worst enemy of spiritual life. So it should be cast out whenever it presents itself.

When we are in the worst of mental states and feel as though we shall never rise again to meet the demands of inner struggle, we are advised to stand behind the mind, and see our mental state as something from which *we* are separate. We should never identify ourselves with any of the mental states, good or bad, for, our real Self, the Ātman, is not the mind.

When in a low state, we must drive out all negative thoughts by repeating to ourself with all our might: 'I am divine, identical with the Supreme Spirit. No misery can ever touch me; I am ever free, infinite and immortal.'[66] Or we can repeat with firm conviction: 'If God be for us who can be against us.'[67] Thus the low state of mind will pass away.

---

[66]Swami Virajananda, *Towards the Goal Supreme* (Calcutta: Advaita Ashrama, 1949), p. 23.

[67]Epistle of St. Paul to the Romans, VIII. 31.

24

EMERGENCY CONTROL DEVICES

It will be within almost everyone's experience that even while earnestly practising the basic disciplines, we come into headlong clash with powerful inimical forces, thoughts, urges, tendencies, and emotions which tend to tear down all our good work in the mind. To deal with such critical situations we have to develop some high-power emergency controls. Like the fire-fighters of a city our methods must be ready at hand day and night.

Patañjali, the teacher of Rāja-Yoga, calls this method *pratipakṣa-bhāvanam*, or thinking contrary thoughts. In the relevant aphorism he says: 'When thoughts obstructive to control of the mind arise, contrary thoughts should be employed.'[68]

For instance, you notice that a big wave of anger is just rising in your mind, which will not only upset your peace for long but cause you great harm. What should you do to neutralize the wave? You have to raise a contrary wave, a wave of love. If lust assails you, you have to raise a contrary wave of purity. This can be done by thinking intensely on the pure heart of a saint.

---

[68] *Yoga-sūtra*, II. 33, 34.

But contrary thoughts have to be raised at the very inception of inimical ones. There is a stage when your anger is just a bubble in your mind; and there is a stage when you are anger itself. Contrary thoughts should be raised when the first bubbles arise; otherwise the method will not work. Contrary thoughts will be powerless when the harmful ones have had time to develop. From this we can understand what a close watch we have to keep on our thoughts and emotions.

It is possible that we may not notice the first few bubbles and may become aware of the situation only when the waves have risen pretty high. What shall we do in this situation? We must tear ourselves away from the situation and go to a lonely place for self-confrontation. There we must catch our mind by the throat, as it were, and say to it: 'O my mind, this will ruin you altogether. Don't you see that?' If we impress the idea forcefully upon the mind, it will behave; for it does not want self-destruction.

When a disciple once asked Swami Brahmananda: What should I do if a distracting thought persistently arises in my mind? He replied:

> 'This thought is immensely harmful to me. It will be my ruin.' Impress this idea again and again upon your mind. The mind will be freed from that distracting thought.

The mind is susceptible to suggestions. It learns whatever you teach it. If through discrimination you can impress upon it the joy and fullness of life in the spirit and the folly of worldly attachments, then your mind will devote itself more and more to God.[69]

Nothing is more exhausting than wrestling with the mind. The more we are exhausted the more turbulent the mind becomes; and ultimately we are swept away. In such a situation a frontal attack on the mind is not very helpful. What should we do then? We should cease to identify ourselves with the mind. If we do this a tremendous work will have been done.

As long as we identify ourselves with the mind we cannot control our minds. The moment we succeed by philosophic thought in separating ourselves from the mind, it has nothing to stand on from where it can make trouble.

But the work in this regard is finished and permanent only when the ignorance of egoism is destroyed. Patañjali defines egoism as the identification of the seer or Ātman with the instruments of seeing, which are the senses, intellect and mind.[70] All our sins and troubles are rooted in this

---

[69]Swami Prabhavananda, op. cit., pp. 135–36.
[70]*Yoga-sūtra*, II. 6.

egoism. Therefore an effective way of controlling the rebellious and wayward state of the mind, is to dissociate ourself from it.

25

DIRECTED THOUGHT

There are other devices which may be effectively employed in an inner emergency created by the sudden onrush of temptation, anger, lust, greed or hatred, succumbing to any one of which may render control of the mind simply impossible.

Teaching what we should do when we watch ourselves being greatly tempted, a Western mystic suggests the following practical measures[71] which can be practised by anyone in distress anywhere in the world. These precepts, with such adaptations as are necessary, will be found helpful in all inner emergencies:

> 1. Follow the example of children when they see a wolf or a bear in the country. They immediately run to the arms of their father or mother or at least they call out to them for help and assistance. Turn in like manner to God, and

---

[71]St. Francis de Sales, *Introduction to the Devout Life* (N.Y., Garden City: Doubleday & Company, 1962), pp. 240–41.

implore His mercy and His help. This is the remedy that our Lord has taught: 'Pray that ye enter not into temptation.'

2. Protest that you will never consent to the temptation; implore His assistance against it; and continue always to protest that you will refuse your consent as long as the temptation shall continue.

3. When you make these protestations and these refusals of consent, do not look the temptation in the face, but look only on our Lord. If you look upon the temptation, especially when it is strong, it may shake your courage.

4. Turn your thought to some good and commendable matter. When good thoughts enter and occupy your heart, they drive away every temptation and evil suggestion.

5. The sovereign remedy against all temptations, whether great or small, is to lay open your heart and communicate its suggestions, feelings and affections to your director (same as Guru).

6. If the temptation should still continue to harass and persecute us after all this, we have nothing to do on our part, but to continue resolute in our protestations never to consent to it. As girls can never be wed as long as they answer no, so the soul, no matter how

long the temptation may last, can never sin as long as she says no.

Psychologically speaking what we need to do in such an inner situation is to calm down the powerful inimical wave which has arisen in the mind. If we ceaselessly call on God, every breath being a call and giving birth to another call, there is then no loophole through which the inimical thought can assert itself and be translated into action. The strategy is to cause a more powerful explosion of helpful thought in order to counteract the explosion of involuntary inimical thought. By constant, even frantic, calling on God or on one's own higher Self, by repetition of a *mantra*, if one is initiated, or of a divine name, a higher impulse will be set going within us to take care of the emergency.

We have to be particularly watchful that though beset by inimical tendencies, we do not give our inner consent to them. Tendencies are not sins. It is the inner consent to wrong tendencies that constitutes sin.

Sri Ramakrishna teaches:

> All the sins of the body fly away if one chants the name of God and sings His glories. The birds of sin dwell in the tree of the body. Singing the name of God is like clapping your

> hands. As, at a clap of the hands, the birds in the tree fly away, so do our sins disappear at the chanting of God's name and glories.[72]

In this homely precept Sri Ramakrishna presents us with a simple remedy for a difficult situation, and this can easily be put into practice by all who are genuinely anxious to get out of it.

In the same vein Swami Brahmananda teaches:

> *Japam, japam, japam*...let the wheel of the name of God go around in the midst of all activities....All the burning of the heart will be soothed. Don't you know how many sinners have become pure and free and divine by taking refuge in the name of God?[73]
>
> Keep a sharp eye on the mind so that no undesirable thought or distractions may enter in. Whenever they try to crowd into your mind, turn it toward God and pray earnestly. Through such practice the mind comes under control and becomes purified.[74]

All the above precepts imply the effectiveness

---

[72]'M'., op. cit., p. 105.
[73]Swami Prabhavananda, op. cit., p. 166.
[74]Ibid., p. 114.

of taking refuge in God. Yet it is necessary to emphasize that those who believe in God, for them the surest remedy in such a situation is to take whole-souled refuge in God. Lay your heart bare before God, and cry a genuine cry for His mercy. The Lord Himself asks the devotee to take refuge in Him and also gives the assurance: 'I will liberate you from all sins';[75] He further declares: 'My devotee will never perish.'[76] Another well-known Hindu scripture attests that the Divine Mother removes the sufferings of all who, being dejected and distressed, take refuge in Her.[77] The same scripture offers adoration to the Divine Mother saying:

> Where *rākṣasas* and snakes of virulent poison (are), where foes and hosts of robbers (exist), where forest conflagrations (occur), there in mid-ocean you stand and save the world.[78]

If this be true—and we believe it to be true—will She not save us when we take refuge in Her in our personal conflagrations?

In the same vein Christ calls to the distressed:

---

[75] *Bhagavad-Gītā*, XVIII. 66.
[76] Ibid., IX. 31.
[77] *Durgā-saptaśati*, XI. 12.
[78] Ibid., XI. 32.

'Come unto Me, all ye that labour and are heavy laden, and I shall give you rest.'[79]

These distinct invitations from the Lord's side are there before the devotee. What sense does it make not to accept this invitation and suffer? For the devotee, therefore, enough and more measures exist for meeting an inner emergency. He has only to put into practice one of the methods or a combination of them suited to his ability and purpose.

The question arises, if a person is a non-believer, what does he do in such inner emergencies as we have been considering?

Let him first tear himself away from the locale of the situation, go out for a brisk long walk in the company of his mind onto something elevating and commendable. If for want of faith he cannot cry to God and lay his inside bare for divine inspection, let him turn to Nature—a flowing river, the sky, the wind, a towering cliff of a mountain, to the vast ocean or the rising sun—and narrate his story *candidly* and ask understanding and power for self-transcendence.

Better than this, however, will be to communicate one's inner situation to a wise, trustworthy selfless man of character and seek his advice and help. Such a person should be very carefully

---

[79]Matthew, XI. 28.

selected. If a trustworthy person is not available, it is better to fight one's inner battle oneself.

What the non-believer should try to do in an emergency is to get out of the mental prison of inner difficulty, into the vastness of the open where he can take wing and leave the turmoil to take care of itself. He must contrive an escape-hatch out of the immediate psychological situation into a larger universe of meaning. This he can perhaps do even by holding on to an inspiring line of a poem or song, or by recalling a great work of art or a few stirring words of a noble mind. One or another of these may serve as a window on eternity for him and enable him to rise to his higher self.

But an escape from an oppressive inner situation, while absolutely necessary as a temporary measure, is neither a final nor a fundamental answer to the problem. For this the non-believer will do well to steadily practise these disciplines of therapeutic and spiritual value taught by Patañjali:

> Or he can try to think deeply on the effulgent light which is beyond all sorrow; or on the heart that has given up all attachments to sense objects; or on anything that appeals to him as good.[80]

---

[80] *Yoga-sūtra*, I. 36, 37, 39.

26

CONTROL OF THOUGHT: THE SECRET

These two sets of disciplines, when practised properly can take care of the conscious level of the mind and also indirectly help the control of the subconscious. The special discipline for urgent operations will function smoothly only in case the general disciplines for basic control are practised.

The most important thing in the general discipline is the control of thought. One who knows how to regulate his thinking will know how to control his mind.

How do we control our thoughts?

Thought-control in the initial stage does not mean that there will be no thought in the mind at all. A thoughtless state may be a stupid state. In the initial stage thought-control means developing the capacity deliberately to think good thoughts and to desist from thinking bad or wrong ones.

In one of his sermons, after preaching in some detail on the method of thought-control, Buddha summarized his teachings:

> Remember, bhikkhus, the only way to become victorious over wrong thoughts is to review from time to time the phases of one's

> mind, to reflect on them, to root out all that is evil and to cultivate all that is good.[81]

Swami Vivekananda teaches:

> We are what our thoughts made us; so take care what you think. Words are secondary. Thoughts live, they travel far. Each thought we think is tinged with our character, so that for the pure and holy man, even his jest or abuse will have the twist of his own love and purity and do good.[82]

This taking 'care of what you think' is so important that we must set about learning how to do it. In other words we must learn how to manufacture good thoughts. If we intend to manufacture good thoughts, we must be careful what food we take, not only by mouth but through all our senses. This we discussed earlier. If the food is pure, our thought will be pure; if the food is impure so will our thought be. It is no use taking wrong food and so making it necessary to struggle to suppress the resultant wrong thoughts. In fact thought-control does not at all mean suppression of thought but mastery of it.

---

[81]Sudhakar Dikshit, op. cit., *Vitakka-Sanātana-Sutta*.

[82]Op. cit. (1964), Vol. VII, p. 14.

In its highest stage thought-control of course means complete cessation of thought. As long as we identify ourselves with the ego or the body we cannot reach this stage. What Swami Vivekananda teaches in the following lesson on *prāṇāyāma* indicates the processes by which cessation of thought is attained:

> ...Identify yourself only with God. After a while thoughts will announce their coming, and we shall learn the way they begin and be aware of what we are going to think, just as on this plane we can look out and see a person coming. This stage is reached when we have learnt to separate ourselves from our minds and see ourselves as one and thought as something apart. Do not let the thoughts grasp you; stand aside and they will die away.
>
> Follow these holy thoughts (of the Chosen Ideal or *Om*); go with them; and when they melt away, you will find the feet of the Omnipotent God. This is the superconscious state; when the idea melts, follow it and melt with it.[83]

We should not, however, be over-zealous to

[83]Op. cit. (1964), Vol. VIII, p. 50.

attain cessation of thought, without practising the disciplines leading to the state. It is better to keep the mind filled with holy thoughts as much as possible, as a result of which the mind will be purified. When purity of mind is attained cessation of thought comes of itself.

Repetition of the *Gāyatrī mantra* greatly helps control of the mind. The meaning of the *mantra* is as follows:

> We meditate upon the adorable effulgence of the resplendent vivifier, Savitṛ; may He stimulate our intellect.[84]

This in effect is a prayer for clarity of understanding, which grows out of purity of mind. The purer the mind, as said before, the easier it is to control.

According to Patañjali, repetition of the sacred *mantra 'Om'* helps the control of the mind in a fundamental way. He teaches:

> He (God) is indicated by the mystic syllable *Om*. The repetition of that *Om* and the contemplation of its import (God) are means of achieving concentration. Thereby is gained

[84] *Ṛg-Veda*, III. 62. 10.

inwardness of thought and freedom from obstacles to concentration.[85]

Inwardness of thought and concentration are gained when the mind is controlled. Commenting on the second and third of these aphorisms of Patañjali, Swami Vivekananda writes:

> Why should there be repetition? We have not forgotten the theory of *saṁskāras*, that the sum total of impressions lives in the mind. They become more and more latent but remain there, and as soon as they get the right stimulus, they come out. Molecular vibration never ceases. When this universe is destroyed, all the massive vibrations disappear; the sun, moon, stars, and earth, melt down; but the vibrations remain in the atoms. Each atom performs the same function as the big worlds do. So even when the vibrations of the *citta* subside, its molecular vibrations go on, and when they get the impulse, come out again. We can now understand what is meant by repetition. It is the greatest stimulus that can be given to the spiritual *saṁskāras*. 'One moment of company with the holy makes a ship

[85] *Yoga-sūtra*, I. 27–29.

to cross this ocean of life.' Such is the power of association. So this repetition of *Om* and thinking of its meaning is keeping good company in your own mind. Study, and then meditate on what you have studied. Thus light will come to you, the Self will become manifest.

But one must think of *Om*, and of its meaning too. Avoid evil company, because the scars of old wounds are in you, and evil company is just the thing that is necessary to call them out. In the same way we are told that good company will call out the good impressions that are in us, but which have become latent. There is nothing holier in the world than to keep good company, because the good impressions will then tend to come to the surface.

The first manifestation of the repetition and thinking of *Om* is that the introspective power will manifest more and more, all the mental and physical obstacles will begin to vanish.[86]

---

[86]Op. cit. (1962), Vol. I, pp. 219–20.

27

CONTROL OF THE SUBCONSCIOUS MIND

It will be hard to demarcate exclusively the conscious and subconscious levels of the mind. Yet for all practical purposes it is found convenient to use such terms for handling the problem under consideration. Discipline meant for controlling the mind on the conscious level cannot leave the subconscious wholly unaffected, and vice versa. What we have discussed so far, however, directly concerns the conscious level.

We now turn to the control of the subconscious mind, as a natural extension of our work on the conscious level. We all have experienced this strange phenomenon in our life: we know what is right but we cannot act up to it; we know what is wrong but we cannot desist from doing it. We make very good resolutions, but before we are aware of it, like the sand-dyke before a tidal wave, they are washed away. We stand bewildered and frustrated.

An examination of this situation will show that we are making resolutions with the conscious part of the mind, and we ourselves are frustrating our resolutions with another part of it, the subconscious, of which we know little. It is an unlighted region of the mind.

The moment we seriously try to control our minds we are beset with inner difficulties. The more we persist, for a time the greater our difficulties may become. In surprise we ask ourselves 'What! am I getting worse day by day and that since taking religion seriously?' We have not to be worried if the situation is like this. This is exactly as it usually is. What happens is this: in the event of deliberately trying to control our conscious mind, we come into clash with the opposing forces of our subconscious mind. These opposing forces are nothing but our stored up *saṁskāras*, past impressions and tendencies. Whatever we think and do leaves a potent impression in our mind. These impressions pop up from the subconscious mind and seek expression and re-manifestation. When they are inconsistent with what we have been thinking with the conscious mind, that causes strife.

The subconscious mind is like the cellar in a house. You do not know how much junk is there, until one day you think you will clear it. As you begin, you are not sure what kind of things and bugs you will encounter. Soon you are tired and leave the work unfinished. So the cellar remains a cellar, it is seldom fit to be a living room. But unless we clear the cellar of the subconscious mind we can never be sure of controlling the conscious mind. Therefore we must find ways of clearing this dark region of the subconscious mind. How do we do it?

Suppose we want to cleanse an ink-pot. How do we do it? We pour clean water into the pot. As the dry ink gets soaked darker water comes out for some time. Then clearer and less inky water comes out. At last we do not find a trace of ink. Clear water poured in causes clear water to come out of the pot.

One of the ways of clearing the subconscious mind is to pour holy thoughts into our mind and allow them to go deep down within ourself. Holy thoughts are like pure water. Only we must not get frightened when we find dark water coming out from within ourselves at a particular stage. If we persist in pouring in holy thoughts, a time will come when we shall find holy thoughts coming out from within. The subconscious mind can then be taken to have been cleared. Control of the conscious mind will not be difficult then.

We must not think that the subconscious is the storehouse of evil only. The subconscious also stores up all our past good and noble thoughts and experiences in seed form. So in the subconscious we do have, stored up, both help for, and opposition to, our efforts at controlling the mind. Our task will be to reduce the opposition and increase the help. Śrī Kṛṣṇa assured Arjuna in the *Gītā*[87] that the yogi who strays away from the path does not come

---

[87] VI. 43.

to eternal grief, for the good work is stored up, and in the next birth he is united with the intelligence acquired in his former body. This union with the intelligence acquired in the previous body can be a powerful unknown factor in this life's attempts at controlling our mind. If this intelligence formerly acquired is to be said to have any particular locus, that locus is the subconscious mind.

So to control the mind, important work needs to be done in the subconscious. On the other hand, if we do not aim at the attainment of life's goal, which is the experience of the superconscious state, we cannot really control our mind, conscious and subconscious. It is only the experience of the superconscious state, or the vision of God, that destroys all the attachments, aversions and delusions, which cause the disturbances and disquiet of the mind.

Our attempts at controlling the mind, therefore, must have reference on the one hand to the subconscious mind and on the other to the superconscious. In other words our entire existence is involved in the process of controlling the mind. Laying stress on the vastness of the task of controlling the mind, Swami Vivekananda points out why our study and efforts cannot remain confined only to the conscious plane:

> The task before us is vast; and first and foremost we must seek to control the vast

> mass of sunken thoughts which have become automatic with us. The evil deed is no doubt on the conscious plane but the cause which produced the evil deed was far beyond in the realms of the unconscious, unseen, and therefore more potent.[88]

He therefore underscores the importance of controlling the 'unconscious'—here no distinction is being made between subconscious and unconscious—for reasons irrefutable. He teaches:

> Practical psychology directs first of all its energies in controlling the unconscious, and we know that we can do it. Why? Because we know the cause of the unconscious is the conscious; the unconscious thoughts are the submerged millions of our old conscious thoughts, old conscious actions become petrified—we do not look at them, do not know them, have forgotten them. But mind you, if the power of evil is in the unconscious, so also is the power of good. We have many things stored in us as in a pocket. We have forgotten them, do not even think of them, and there are many of them, rotting, becoming positively dangerous; they

---

[88] Op. cit. (1963), Vol. II, p. 34.

> come forth, the unconscious causes which kill humanity. True psychology would, therefore, try to bring them under the control of the conscious. The great task is to revive the whole man, as it were, in order to make him the complete master of himself. Even what we call the automatic action of the organs within our bodies such as the liver etc., can be made to obey our commands.[89]

But control of the 'unconscious' does not accomplish the entire task on hand. There is more to it. So Swami Vivekananda teaches:

> This is the first part of the study, the control of the unconscious. The next is to go beyond the conscious. Just as unconscious work is beneath consciousness, so there is another work which is above consciousness. When this superconscious state is reached man becomes free and divine; death becomes immortality, weakness becomes infinite power, and iron bondage becomes liberty. That is the goal, the infinite realm, of the superconscious.[90]

To clinch his teaching on this subject he says:

---

[89]Ibid., p. 35.
[90]Ibid., p. 35.

So, therefore, we see now that there must be a twofold work. First, by the proper working the *iḍā* and the *piṅgalā*, which are the two existing ordinary currents, to control the subconscious action; and secondly, to go beyond even consciousness.

The books say that he alone is the yogi who, after long practice in self-concentration, has attained to this truth. The *suṣumṇā* now opens and a current which never before entered into this new passage will find its way into it, and gradually ascend to (what we call in figurative language) the different lotus centres, till at last it reaches the brain. Then the yogi becomes conscious of what he really is, God Himself.[91]

The reference here is to the awakening of *kuṇḍalinī* through the Rāja-Yoga method of *prāṇāyāma*, which is an aid in the control of one's mind. *Prāṇāyāma*, however, as we have mentioned before, is to be learnt personally from an expert teacher who is not easy to find. Those who are continent and earnest aspirants and who are fortunate to have such a teacher, may well learn from him and their task of controlling the mind will be easier. But

---

[91]Ibid., pp. 35–36.

the greater number of those who struggle with their mind and want to control it may neither live in a very congenial atmosphere for practising *prāṇāyāma,* for example in a smog-filled modern city, nor have the opportunity of learning the discipline from an expert teacher. Most of them, therefore, must depend upon other disciplines which can be as effective if practised with faith and diligence. Repetition of *Om* while meditating on its meaning is the most efficacious of these practices.

When the *kuṇḍalinī,* the latent spiritual power, is awakened in a person, the control of the subconscious mind, which is hard to handle, is taken care of. But, in fact, the Rāja-Yoga method of awakening the *kuṇḍalinī* cannot be easily practised by the vast majority of people.

Fortunately, there are other disciplines through the practice of which one's spiritual consciousness can be awakened.

Sri Ramakrishna teaches: 'One's spiritual consciousness is not awakened by merely reading books. One should also pray to God. The *kuṇḍalinī* is roused if the aspirant feels restless for God.[92]

'...The *kuṇḍalinī* is speedily awakened if one follows the path of *bhakti.*'[93]

---

[92]'M', op. cit., p. 814.

[93]Ibid., p. 310.

One day a disciple asked Swami Brahmananda, 'Sir, how can the *kuṇḍalinī* be roused?'

The Swami replied:

> According to some there are some exercises, but I believe it can be best done through repetition of the Divine Name and meditation. Specially suited to our age is the practice of *japam* or constant repetition of God's name and meditation upon it. There is no spiritual practice easier than this. But meditation must accompany the repetition of the *mantra* (the mystic word).[94]

Thus, by the practice of the spiritual disciplines of the path of *bhakti*, such as prayer, repetition of the Divine Name, and meditation, our spiritual potency is awakened. And this awakened power easily takes care of the difficulties of the subconscious mind. So no one need be in despair thinking that because he is unable to practise Rāja-Yoga disciplines his way to controlling the subconscious mind is closed. No, it is not, for there is none so helpless in this world that he cannot repeat the Divine Name. If there is, his time for controlling the mind is not yet.

---

[94]Swami Prabhavananda, op. cit., p. 149.

28

BEWARE OF A TRICK OF THE MIND

We must know that the mind sometimes plays a trick on itself, that is to say, the subconscious mind on the conscious. When we are struggling with temptation or weakness on the conscious level, suddenly the picture of a more difficult situation flashes before our mind's eye, and fear-stricken we wonder: 'What shall I do if I am beset with such difficulties?' In worrying about our future, our present topples over. Being off guard, we are swept away by the present temptation.

How do we prevent this sabotage? We can do so by simply clarifying our idea of time. As Meister Eckhart, the German mystic, says: 'In the heart of this moment is eternity.' We must clearly see that every moment is only *this moment*. If we have taken care of this moment, we have taken care of our entire future. If we do not submit to temptation only for this moment, and always only for this moment, we never shall submit to it.

Therefore, whatever situation we may be in, let us stand firm in our resolution this moment, and we shall succeed. The future is nothing but Māyā. It is foolishness to worry about the future while allowing the devil to conquer the present.

The challenge of spiritual life is very simple: to be good, truly moral and master of ourselves for only this moment. What time is there outside this moment, that we should worry about it?

29

BELIEVERS ARE AT AN ADVANTAGE IN CONTROLLING THE MIND

Those who believe in God have a distinct advantage over those who do not believe, as far as mind-control is concerned. When faith in God is sincerely cultivated, we get potent help for controlling the mind. Through the practice of devotion, zeal for God is developed; and this zeal for God can work wonders by way of removing obstructions to the control of the mind. In the words of Sri Ramakrishna:

> As the tiger devours other animals, so does the 'tiger of the zeal for the Lord' eat up lust, anger and other passions. Once this zeal grows in the heart, lust and the other passions disappear. The *gopīs* of Vrindavan had that state of mind because of their zeal for Kṛṣṇa.[95]

[95]'M', op. cit., p. 140.

When lust, anger and other passions disappear the mind becomes purified. A pure mind is easily controlled. But the non-believer will have to work at it the hard and long way, for, unless he gives up his unbelief, he cannot develop zeal for God.

Śrī Kṛṣṇa teaches:

> Even a devotee (not to speak of a saint) of Mine who is not the master of his senses and is troubled by sense-objects, is generally not overcome by them owing to his powerful devotion.[96]

The psychological process through which purity of mind comes to the believer is simple. When he develops love for God, his mind dwells on Him, for we naturally concentrate on whatever we love. We assimilate the qualities of whatever we concentrate our mind on. Therefore when we concentrate our mind on God, we assimilate what the *Gītā* calls *daivī sampad,* divine qualities.[97] Purity of heart, control of the senses, absence of anger, tranquillity, absence of fickleness are some of the divine qualities which a true lover of God gets without deliberately striving for them. In other words he attains control of the mind in a spontaneous way.

---

[96] *Śrīmad Bhāgavatam*, XI. 14–18.

[97] XVI. 1, 2.

30

THE SIMPLEST AND THE SUREST METHOD OF CONTROLLING THE MIND

We have said a few things about methods of controlling the mind. But one truth will bear repetition. And this truth is laid much stress upon both by Sri Ramakrishna and Holy Mother. Sri Ramakrishna teaches:

> The best thing for people whose minds are attracted by sense-objects is to cultivate the dualistic attitude and chant loudly the name of the Lord as enjoined in the *Nārada Pañcarātra*.[98]

On another occasion Sri Ramakrishna said to a devotee:

> Through the path of devotion subtle senses come readily and naturally under control. Carnal pleasures become more and more insipid as divine love grows in your heart. Can the pleasures of the body attract the husband and the wife on the day their child has died?
>
> Devotee: But I have not learnt to love God?

---

[98] *Sayings of Sri Ramakrishna*, saying 349.

Sri Ramakrishna: Take His name constantly. This will cleanse all sin, lust and anger, and all desires for the pleasures of the body will vanish.

Devotee: But I do not find delight in His name.

Sri Ramakrishna: Then pray with a yearning heart that He may teach you to relish His name. Undoubtedly He will grant your prayer…'I find no delight in Thy name!'— If a delirious patient loses all taste for food, you must despair of his life. But if he relishes food even slightly, you may hope for his recovery. So I say, 'Find joy in His name'. Durgā, Kṛṣṇa, Śiva—any name will do. And if you daily feel greater attraction for taking His name and a greater joy in it, you need fear no more. The delirium must be cured, and His grace will surely descend on you.[99]

The same truth comes to us equally forcefully from Holy Mother's life and teaching:

The mother was seated on her bed. The disciple was reading to her letters written by her devotees. The letters contained such

[99]Ibid., saying 350.

statements as: 'The mind cannot be controlled etc.' The Holy Mother listened to these and said in rather an animated voice, 'The mind will be steadied if one repeats the name of God fifteen to twenty thousand times a day. It is truly so. I myself have experienced it. Let them practise it first; if they fail, let them complain. One should practise *japam* with some devotion, but this is not done. They will not do anything; they will only complain saying "Why do I not succeed"?'[100]

An easier and more potent method of controlling the mind than the one explained by Holy Mother is not known to man. But one must be simple in heart to accept and practise it. Let us test these words of the Holy Mother for ourselves and see whether or not they come true in our lives.

But this warning should be given that for a beginner to repeat the name of the Lord twenty thousand times a day suddenly, may not be advisable. One should begin modestly and through regular practice steadily increase the number under the guidance of the Guru. The most important thing is to begin doing something in the right direction now.

---

[100]Swamis Tapasyananda and Nikhilananda, *Sri Sarada Devi: The Holy Mother* (Chennai: Sri Ramakrishna Math, 1949), p. 489.

Earnest prayer to God every day at regular hours for good intentions and purity of the mind—which is the same as the controlled state of mind—will greatly help. Sincere prayers are answered, says Sri Ramakrishna.

As our practice of prayer grows in intensity one result will ensue. Gradually we shall notice that the character of our prayer has been changing: it has become more God-centred than object-centred. We have become more interested in God than in what we want from Him. Asking has been transmuted into love of God. It is this love of God which is the most important factor in controlling the mind.

In the beginning this love may appear to be absent in our hearts, or very faint even if it is there. But through various methods—such as holy company, repetition of the Lord's name, study of the lives and teachings of saints, ritualistic worship, devotional singing—this love may gradually grow in us. As it becomes a strong force within us, we easily overcome inimical inner forces which cause non-control of the mind. A time comes in a person's life when the mind spontaneously gravitates towards the object of supreme love. In such a state of mind bliss is experienced. When we are confirmed in this state we shall have attained the controlled state of mind automatically.

So the most complete answer to the question,

How to control the mind? is: Love God. But if you do not believe in God, then believe in yourself. Exercise your will and transcend the *guṇas* by self-effort. By this means also you will gain control of your mind.

In any case, for the believer as for the non-believer, a way of controlling the mind always remains open. There is no greater blessing in life than a controlled state of mind. Let us do our very best to acquire it, for this will lead us to the greatest of blessings.

❋ ❋ ❋

A SUMMARY

Mind-control has always been a difficult task even for a heroic person; but it is not an impossible one. There are well-defined methods.

The entire secret of controlling the mind is given by Śrī Kṛṣṇa in the two words *abhyāsa* and *vairāgya*, practice and dispassion.

To bring these two disciplines into the stream of our life: we have to develop a strong will to control the mind; we have to understand the nature of our mind; we have to learn certain techniques and practise them.

In order to strengthen the will, we need to overcome our pleasure-motive and also understand what is involved in controlling the mind.

The nature of the mind is explained from the Hindu point of view in *The Complete Works of Swami Vivekananda*.

To be able to control our mind we must know how not to make our task unnecessarily difficult.

Mind-control is the personal task of the person concerned. The object of mind-control is the realization of our absolute oneness with the Divine. For this no price can be too great to pay.

To be able to practise effectively the disciplines leading to mind-control we need a favourable inner climate. This includes the capacity to accept certain features of life as inevitable.

For controlling the mind we need two sets of inner disciplines: one to give a healthy general direction to the mind, and the other to save us in emergencies.

The purer the mind, the easier it is to control. So we should practise disciplines for the purification of the mind. Our object should be to bring about a preponderance of *sattva* in our inner nature, and then to transcend *sattva* by purifying it according to authentic disciplines.

The easiest method of doing this, however, is cultivating holy company.

The Vedantic disciplines can be helpfully supplemented by the Yoga disciplines taught by Patañjali.

Along with the practice of the disciplines of Yoga should go the practice of discrimination. Then we shall be able to train the mind to behave. When it has been trained to behave, the senses will have been trained not to come in contact with their objects, but to obey the mind. Then *pratyāhāra* will have been achieved.

Certain ancillary measures which greatly help the effective practice of the main disciplines should be given attention. These measures are: keeping our human relationships in order; giving the mind a healthy occupation; making right use of the imagination; and guarding against despondency.

Mind-control is greatly helped by the practice of meditation, and meditation by mind-control.

In explosive inner situations to apply high-power emergency brakes, Patañjali's teaching is: practise thinking contrary thoughts. Ceaseless chanting of the Lord's name and also taking refuge in God's help.

Methodical control of thought is a great secret in controlling the mind.

Without controlling the subconscious, the mind cannot be controlled. The subconscious can be controlled by pouring holy thought into it, as it were, and by the practice of *prāṇāyāma* and other disciplines, among which is *bhakti*. These rouse the *kuṇḍalinī*, the latent spiritual power in a person.

We must beware of a harmful kind of imagination. By being truly moral only for this moment, and then at the next moment for the next moment, and so on always we can guard against such a possibility.

Believers are at an advantage in controlling the mind.

The simplest and surest method of controlling the mind is through love of God.

Those who do not believe in God can control the mind by transcending the *guṇas* through self-effort.

Mind-control is valuable because it leads to the highest blessing—the illumined state of being.

❄ ❄❄

GLOSSARY

Arjuna The great hero of the Hindu epic, *Mahābhārata*. Friend and disciple of Śrī Kṛṣṇa. It was to him that Śrī Kṛṣṇa taught the *Bhagavad-Gītā* on the battlefield Kurukṣetra.

Ātman A term of Vedanta Philosophy, denoting the Self or Soul; refers also to the Supreme Spirit (Brahman) which according to Non-dualistic (Advaita) Vedanta, is one with the individual soul.

Atharva-Veda One of the four Vedas, the most sacred scriptures of the Hindus. The other three are: Ṛk, Sāma, Yajus.

Avidyā A term of Vedanta Philosophy denoting primal ignorance, individual or cosmic. According to Nondualistic Vedanta, it is responsible for the perception of multiplicity. The beginning of this ignorance cannot be traced, but it comes to an end for a person when he attains Self-knowledge.

Bhagavad-Gītā The well-known Hindu scripture, which occurs in the Bhīṣma parva of the *Mahābhārata*.

Bhagavān The Lord of the Universe. Also used as an honorific before the names of great world-teachers or persons of extraordinary spiritual excellence.

Bhakti Devotion, attachment, loyalty, faithfulness to God.

Bhikkhu A religious mendicant. Commonly used to refer to a Buddhist monk.

Brahmā The creator God of the Hindu Trinity. The other two being Viṣṇu and Śiva.

Brahman The Absolute. The supreme Reality of Nondualistic Vedanta. See 'Ātman'.

Holy Mother Denotes Sri Sarada Devi (1853–1920), the holy spouse of Sri Ramakrishna.

Iḍā A 'nerve current' (in Yoga terminology) in the spinal column. See *Piṅgalā* and *Suṣumṇā*.

Jñāni A spiritual aspirant who follows the Nondualistic path of knowledge and discrimination to realize the highest Truth.

Kṛṣṇa, Śrī An Incarnation of God; the celebrated hero of Hindu mythology; the popular Hindu deity; and the world-teacher who taught the *Bhagavad-Gītā*. His life and acts are narrated in the *Śrīmad Bhāgavatam* and the *Mahābhārata*.

Kuṇḍalinī The spiritual energy lying dormant in every individual, which can be awakened through appropriate spiritual exercises.

Mahārāj Literally, a great king. Also used as an honorific in addressing monks in India.

Mantra, A Word formula (or prayer) sacred to a deity, and a sound-symbol of the deity, by devoted and reverential repetition of which the deity is spiritually realized.

Māyā A term of Vedanta philosophy denoting cosmic ignorance which obscures Reality and conjures up the universe of multiplicity.

Niyama Literally, restraints, check. In Yoga disciplines *niyama* is the second of the eight principal steps for the attainment of perfection in Yoga.

Om The most sacred of all words, being the Word out of which emanated the universe. The symbol of both the personal God and the Absolute. *Om* is regarded by the Hindus as the greatest *mantra,* being of incalculable spiritual potency.

Patañjali The founder of one of the six systems of Indian philosophy, namely Yoga philosophy. The celebrated author of the *Yoga-sūtra.* According to some scholars he flourished about 150 B.C.

Piṅgalā A 'nerve current' in the spinal column referred to in Yoga terminology. See *Suṣumṇā*

Prakṛti Primordial nature; the material substratum of creation. It consists of three substantive forces (*guṇas*), namely, *sattva, rajas,* and *tamas.*

Rājasika Having predominance of the quality of *rajas* (a term explained in the text of the book).

Rāja-Yoga One of the four main ancient Hindu spiritual disciplines. This system of discipline, ascribed to Patañjali, deals with the methods of realizing the highest Truth through concentration of mind.

Ramakrishna, Sri The world-teacher of India regarded as a divine Incarnation. A.D. 1836–1886.
Ṛk-Veda One of the four Vedas, the most sacred scriptures of the Hindus.
Sāma-Veda One of the four Vedas.
Sanatkumāra A celebrated figure of Hindu mythology. One of the four mind-born sons of Brahmā, the creator God. They are highly regarded as spiritual persons. The other three are Sanaka, Sanātana, and Sanandana.
Śrīmad Bhāgavatam A scripture of the Hindus dealing with the life and teachings of Śrī Kṛṣṇa.
Suṣumṇā A 'nerve' running through the centre of the spinal column, extending from the base of the spine to the brain. It is through the *suṣumṇā* that spiritual energy rises when the *kuṇḍalinī* is awakened.
Tāmasika Having preponderance of the quality of *tamas* (a term explained in the text of the book).
Upaniṣads The celebrated scriptures of the Hindus.
Vedas The most sacred scriptures of the Hindus; the ultimate authority of Hindu religion and philosophy.
Vedanta Literally the concluding portion of the Vedas or their essence. One of the six systems of Indian philosophy, discussed mainly in the Upaniṣads, the *Bhagavad-Gītā* and the *Brahma-sūtra*, ascribed to Vyāsa.

Vivekananda, Swami A disciple of Sri Ramakrishna. Vivekananda (1863–1902), was a world-teacher who carried the message of Vedanta to the West in the nineties of the 19th century. He also awakened the Indian nation by his Vedantic preaching, and substantially contributed to its renaissance in a number of ways.

Yama Literally, restraining, controlling, curbing. The first of the eight steps leading to the attainment of Yoga, as taught by Patañjali.

Yoga Union of the individual soul with the Supreme Spirit. The term also denotes the methods of attaining this union.

Yogi One who practises the disciplines leading to union with Supreme Spirit. Also denotes one who has attained such union.

❋ ❋ ❋